OPTIONS TRADING CRASH COURSE

A FULL IMMERSION GUIDE FOR BEGINNERS AND EXPERTS TO MAKE MONEY IN 7 DAYS. LEARN TRADERS' PSYCHOLOGY, ALGORITHMIC TRADING, AND THE BEST STRATEGIES TO TRADE OPTIONS

Benjamin Ray Bears

© **Copyright 2021 by Benjamin Ray Bears - All rights reserved**.

This document is geared towards providing exact and reliable information in regard to the topic and issue covered.

- From a Declaration of Principles which was accepted and approved equally by a Committee of the American Bar Association and a Committee of Publishers and Associations.

In no way is it legal to reproduce, duplicate, or transmit any part of this document in either electronic means or in printed format. All rights reserved.

The information provided herein is stated to be truthful and consistent, in that any liability, in terms of inattention or otherwise, by any usage or abuse of any policies, processes, or directions contained within is the solitary and utter responsibility of the recipient reader. Under no circumstances will any legal responsibility or blame be held against the publisher for any reparation, damages, or monetary loss due to the information herein, either directly or indirectly.

Respective authors own all copyrights not held by the publisher.

The information herein is offered for informational purposes solely and is universal as so. The presentation of the information is without contract or any type of guarantee assurance.

The trademarks that are used are without any consent, and the publication of the trademark is without permission or backing by the trademark owner. All trademarks and brands within this book are for clarifying purposes only and are owned by the owners themselves, not affiliated with this document.

Table of Contents

INTRODUCTION 7

CHAPTER 1: TAKING THE RISK 11

CHAPTER 2: WHAT IS AN OPTION? 13

CHAPTER 3: WHY OPTIONS RATHER THAN STOCKS? 21

CHAPTER 4: WHY IS OPTIONS TRADING WORTH THE RISK? 24

CHAPTER 5: TRADING PSYCHOLOGY 32

CHAPTER 6: CLASSIC MISTAKES TO AVOID 37

CHAPTER 7: COMMON PITFALLS IN OPTIONS TRADING 46

CHAPTER 8: HOW TO GET STARTED IN OPTIONS TRADING 54

CHAPTER 9: THE ROLE OF THE UNDERLYING STOCK 63

CHAPTER 10: UNDERSTANDING THE STRIKE PRICE 66

CHAPTER 11: BASIC AND ADVANCE TRADING – SELLING COVERED CALLS 69

CHAPTER 12: BENEFITS AND RISKS OF COVERED CALLS 73

CHAPTER 13: OUTCOMES OF A COVERED CALL SELL 78

CHAPTER 14: STEPPING UP A TIER: BUYING CALLS 85

CHAPTER 15: STRATEGIES FOR BUYING CALLS 91

CHAPTER 16: UNDERSTANDING VOLATILITY 94

CHAPTER 17: HOW TO BUY AND SELL PUTS 102

CHAPTER 18: STRATEGIES FOR NEW OPTIONS TRADERS 110

CHAPTER 19: RISK MANAGEMENT 119

CHAPTER 20: THE GREEKS 126

CHAPTER 21: ALGORITHMIC TRADING 133

CONCLUSION 139

Introduction

There is often confusion about why traders choose options when stocks and bonds do just fine. What some tend to miss out on is the vast difference in the earnings potential. Stocks generally return a profit of 8%–12% per annum, which is pretty impressive in and of it. However, options are a lot more lucrative with a much larger potential.

Firstly, options' flexibility allows them to be traded based on a wide variety of underlying securities. The variety and range of options strategies are massive. Also, the spreads provide real flexibility in the manner in which they can be traded. Traders have flexibility and versatility in limiting the risks of assuming market positions when it comes to hedging. Even simply trying to benefit from stock movements, there are numerous opportunities available.

Some options trades typically generate profits upwards of 50%. Making 100% profits within a short period and even more, is not unheard of. This is why a lot of experienced traders choose options. They are extremely lucrative and highly profitable. It is also possible to make money trading options in any market condition. Traders can make money when the market is bullish, bearish, and even when it is stagnant. As such, you do not need specific market conditions, and hence profitability throughout the year is possible.

Experts agree that trading options offer plenty of benefits that are not offered by other types of securities. While not all traders may want to engage in options trading, there are certain aspects of it that other traders find attractive.

Potential for Astronomical Profits

One of the main reasons for trading options is the opportunity of making significantly large profits compared to all other forms of trade in the markets. This is possible even without large sums of money. The principle behind this approach is leverage. A trader needs not to have large amounts of funds to earn huge profits. For instance, with as little as $10,000, it is possible to earn amounts such as $300,000 or even $800,000 simply using leverage.

Take the example of a trader whose trading fund is $10,000. The trader wishes to invest this amount in Company ABC. Now the current stock price is $20 though this price is expected to rise. The trader could use the funds to purchase the shares directly and receive 500 shares for their money. If the stock price were to rise to $25 within a month, the trader would have made $5 per share or a total of $2,500 in profits.

Alternatively, the trader could purchase call options of XYZ stocks with the same amount of money. The options allow the trader to purchase back the underlying stocks within a certain period. Now, options contracts cost between $1 and $4 depending on certain factors, such as the underlying security value. In our example, one call options costs $2 so for the $10,000, the trader receives 5,000 options contracts.

If the trader chooses to exercise the right to sell the underlying shares in the next month, they stand to profit from $5 per share. Remember that they have a right to a total of 5,000 shares for a total profit of $25,000. This demonstrates the capacity and power of options and how profitable this kind of trade can be.

Versatility and Flexibility

Another extremely appealing benefit of trading in options is the inherent flexibility. Options offer lots of flexibility with dozens of different strategies to pursue. This compares well with numerous other trade and investment options out there. Most of these do not offer as much flexibility as options do. Also, most other securities have limited strategies, limiting the flexibility that a trader has on that security.

Take stocks, for instance. Even stock traders encounter certain limitations that are not inherent in options trading. There are plenty of strategies ranging from simple to compound to complex strategies. Stock traders generally buy, hold, or sell stocks. This contrasts greatly with options because of the tens of strategies available to them. The versatility and flexibility inherent in options trading far surpass that of most other securities.

Great Risk vs. Reward Consideration

Like all good traders, it is essential to weigh the risk posed by a certain trade compared to the possible rewards. When trading using options, the style adapted will indicate the type of risk inherent in the trade. The above example clearly shows how profitable the options trading process is. If a loss were to be incurred in the above instance, then the total loss would have been the options' cost.

In this case, the risk is worth the reward because the amount expected to be lost negligible compared to the gain to be made. In general, the higher the risk than the higher the potential return. Any time a trader considers a trade, then the risk versus reward ratio should be considered.

Chapter 1: Taking the Risk

Risk in Options Trading

Risk is at the heart of all types of investment, as without it, there would be a need for reward. As such, options trading is risky at the best of times, even for those who might be considered experts and certainly for those who are still new to the field. Luckily, there are certainly ways to mitigate that risk as many of the major pitfalls of options trading have been well documented by those who have come before. What's more, they have also been distilled down and classified so that all you need to do is memorize the following and ensure that you do your best not to let it intrude on your trading success.

It doesn't matter what type of trade you are working with, the first thing you are going to want to do is to consider three main things. First, you will want to be aware of how much a specific price will likely change before the option's expiration in question. From there, you will want to determine how volatile the underlying asset is and how much time the option has to turn you a profit before its expiration. When you are purchasing options, it is important to identify the direction you expect the underlying stock to move in and how long you expect it to continue to move in the specified direction. In these instances, the amount of time still available won't be as important when it comes to ensuring the overall maximum value.

To ensure that risk is minimized, it is important to keep in mind that the best strategies focus on either high positive risk value or high negative risk value—there is little value in betting on the middle ground. Remember, some option types are always going to end up being more profitable than others in specific scenarios—you just need to have the patience and the foresight to know what's coming before it gets here. With that being said, however, it is important to always keep in mind that statistical projections cannot tell the future, which means that any analysis that is done is strictly hypothetical. Never invest more money into a particular trade, no matter how reliable it seems, than you can ultimately afford to lose.

When it comes to making trades in groups or combining them in other ways, it is important to consider the net risk of the entire trade instead of focusing on the specific risk likelihoods of parts of the whole. This will make it easier for you to determine the most profitable way to move forward at any juncture because it makes the risk/reward split much easier to analyze. Remember, there are multiple types of risk which means that understanding what each means for your specific trade is crucial to covering all your bases and making successful options trades on a reliable basis.

Chapter 2: What is an Option?

Trading options is much like trading stocks, though there are significant differences. There are two major categories of options (calls and puts): agreements that grant the bearer the fundamental right, such as a stock, to buy or sell the underlying security. However, options are traded on exchanges just as stocks are. Individual investors may use a brokerage company to place buying and selling requests.

Options are precious as they can improve a person's portfolio by adding revenue, offering power, and even protection, they do so. Usually, there is a selection of options tailored to an investor's interest, depending on the situation. A more straightforward example would be to practice options as an active defense against a weakening stock market to mitigate downside risks. Options may also be used to produce recurring revenue. Sometimes, they are used for hypothetical purposes, including making bets on the direction of the stock.

It is not unusual to invest in options. The first options contract, in reality, debuted in 1973 on the Chicago Board Options Exchange. Although today's option is still close to what it was, a lot has changed. The company size in terms of creditors, exchange rates, and exchange contracts is the most crucial distinction; this has grown exponentially. More trading options are now available than ever.

Investors use options for particular purposes. Mainly, a call option is a contract granting the holder the right to purchase a stock at a defined price for a specific period. If they expect a more drastic change in the share price, some investors buy calls. Others will sell calls if a stock price is anticipated to flat-trade or to shift lower.

You need to learn what they are first to trade options. An option is a contract related to a specific stock or other investment between a buyer and a seller. The option buyer has the right to compel the option seller within the time-limit set by the agreement to do as the contract specifies. The seller must meet the option's instructions until the buyer has exercised the option.

The options adhere to the broader group of securities classified as derivatives. A derivative's value depends on or is determined from something else's value. A stock option is a stock derivative. Options are financial equity derivatives; their value depends on the price of some other asset. Calls, Puts, Options, Forwards, Swaps, and Mortgage-backed securities, among others, are examples of derivatives.

What is Options Trading?

Options are agreements that grant the bearer the right, and not the duty, to either sell or buy the sum of any underlying asset at a fixed price at or before the contract's expiry. Options may be purchased from mutual investment accounts, like any other asset class.

Investors necessitate brokerage accounts to invest in people who expect that their original investment will turn into life-changing wealth for the stock. But it's essential to select a broker that gives you direct exposure to all the different kinds of exciting investments. While most brokers will meet basic needs, those who want to take advantage of advanced investment strategies need to be careful in choosing brokers who can give them the opportunity to trade and the resources they need in those areas to make the right options.

Stock options are not as difficult as people would make them seem. People tend to make it sound complex at times, but it is a simple thing that almost everyone can understand. Do not stop yourself as a novice from thinking that trading options are an emotional investment. You will be surprised at how simple and straightforward it is and wonder why you've never invested in it before. There are four factors which investors should consider when investing in stock options. If these factors are taken into account, this would have a positive effect on your trade.

One chance to turn the trade is to look at the options market. Trading options are very different from trading mutual funds or bonds, but they can have many enormous advantages for investors. Below, you can look at precisely what trading options are and how they can benefit you.

The most significant thing regarding an option is that the buyer of an option has the power to pursue the contract, as its name implies, but is under no pressure to do so. Hence, only if it is wise to do so, the Buyer of Option can use this right. Assume in the following example that the Call Option allowed the buyer to pay $200 per share for a specific stock. Suppose the stock is sold on the open market for $100 a share. In that case, the option holder will never exercise the option since it would be dumb to pay $200 on the free market under the promise of a share that the buyer might purchase for $100. However, if the market share price was $275, then the buyer could exercise the right, as $200 would be a steal over the share price commonly owned.

For example, a stock call option provides the buyer of the option the right to purchase a specific number of shares at a given price at any time before the stated expiry date. If the buyer exercises the right, the seller of the option must sell the stock to the buyer.

Amongst those top picks for you, find the best stockbroker. There's a stockbroker to meet your business needs if you are looking for an exclusive sign-up offer, excellent customer service, $0 commissions, intuitive smartphone applications, or more.

There are several different trading options. In addition to the call options stated above, put options give the buyer option the right to sell stock at a given price, thus protecting the buyer option from stock losses. To take advantage of more sophisticated approaches to options that can make a profit in various cases, you can also combine various call and put options.

A contract that gives the investor the right to sell or buy an asset at a fixed agreed strike price at a specified date depending on the form of option, while not an obligation, we can quickly identify stock options now that we know the definition of both stocks and options. We may describe the term as follows: stock options offer an owner the right at a given price and date to sell or buy a stock.

The stock option may also refer to an incentive in the form of an opportunity offered by a business to any employee to buy shares in a company at a predetermined fixed price or a discount.

Stock options have become a source of concern in recent years. We are seeing more and more individuals interested in options for trading. Some think it's a scam; others say it's not a worthwhile investment, while others say it's not a worthwhile investment. All these speculations lead us in one direction, namely, understanding what stock options are. We are going to have to go over stock options very carefully to answer this question correctly. We'll need to know more about it and what it means. This experience makes it simpler, instead of using theories, to make decisions with facts. You should never back up something you will get to tell you. Having awareness gives you an added value and puts you in the right spot.

Knowledge gathering will alter your trading skills as an inexperienced trader. It will make you an expert in the trade to acquire the necessary abilities and knowledge within a matter of time. Before you commit to a stock option, this book will give you the information you need. It is nice that you have taken the first step towards getting this book. It demonstrates that you are ready and eager to know, and that is a big step. Learning to apply it is essential; apart from gaining skills, you will do what you have learned. Most individuals receive data but are unable to make successful use of it for their benefit. In addition to acquiring expertise, having to learn to apply is necessary. It is going to mean doing what you heard. Many individuals collect data but are unable to make equal use of it for their benefit. We hope you will have the courage to trade a stock option after you read the book. The book focuses on beginners in particular and is intended to make a difference in their lives.

The Options Jargons

Being familiar with Options Trading needs some vocabulary to remember. The basics for starting up to trade options are here.

Strike Price

The strike price would have to be calculated to know whether a stock could be exercised. When an alternative arrives at the expiry date, there is a meaning that it is expected to have; this may be lower or higher than the stock price, which we refer to as an associated asset's strike price. You can buy a Call Option at a fixed price for the strike if you expect the investment cost to rise as an investor. The value of a call will become the price beyond which the holder of the option will sell an asset if the bid expires when placing calls. Maybe the strike price, too, will be the exercise price. It is a crucial aspect to recognize when assessing the significance of the alternative. Depending on when the options are exercised, the strike price may vary. As an investor, it is a great approach to keep watching the strike price to explain its success.

The Right, but Not the Liability

What comes to mind immediately when this sentence is being read? Yeah, we say that you can purchase any product when we talk or have rights. We refer to the fact that one has no legal authority to perform an obligation when we speak about responsibility. Options do not grant a lawful right to perform a mission to traders, this indicates that the right of trade is there, but the statute does not enforce it.

Contracts

Contracts refer to the number of shares required to be purchased by individuals. An asset class of one hundred shares corresponds to a contract. When determining the value of the stock before the expiry date, contracts ought to be dignified. After the expiry date, a contract can be counted as void. Understanding this will allow you to find the right moment to work out a contract. For a case in which somebody buys ten options, an investor gets ten calls for $350. Suppose stock prices go past $ 350 at the expiry rate. In that case, the dealer receives an opportunity to buy or sell 1000 stock shares at $ 350: this occurs at the same moment, regardless of the stock's price. The option expires uselessly in a situation where the stock is below $350. That will result in a complete loss as an investor. You will lose the whole amount you used to buy the options, and you will not get it back. Be aware of the contracts and exercise them on outstanding trading results if you consider engaging in trading options.

Chapter 3: Why Options Rather than Stocks?

Trading options and trading stocks are different because stocks and options have different characteristics. Stocks represent shares of ownership in individual companies or options. This allows the stock trader to bet in any direction that they feel the stock price is headed.

Stocks are a great investment if you think of long-term yields, such as for retirement and have the capital. They are very simplistic in the approach in that the trader buys the stock and wagers on the price that he or she thinks will rise at a certain time in the future. The hope is that the price will increase in value, thus gaining the trader a substantial yield.

Stocks are also a great option for those who want to invest without keeping a steady eye on the growth of the investment.

The risk of investing in stocks is that stocks' prices can plummet to zero at any moment. This means that the investor can lose his or her entire investment at the drop of a hat because stocks are very volatile from one day to the next. They are very reactive to world events such as wars, politics, scandals, epidemics, and natural disasters.

On the other hand, options are an excellent option for traders who would like flexibility with timing and risks. The trader is under no obligation and can see how the trade plays out over the time specified by the option contract. In that period, the price is locked, which is also a great appeal.

Trading options also require a lower investment compared to stocks typically.

Another great appeal for options reading is that the specified period is typically shorter than investing in stocks. This allows for regular buying and selling as options have different expiration dates. Expiration dates can range from just a few days to several years.

The drawback that makes some people hesitate in trading options is that it is more complex than trading stocks. The trader needs to learn new jargon and vocabulary such as strike prices, calls and puts to determine how to set up effective options. Not only does the trader have to learn new terms, but he or she also has to develop new skillsets and the right mindset for options trading.

Another advantage of options rather than stocks is that it allows the trader to hedge their investment if they are worried about sudden price fluctuations. Options contracts allow for the trader to buy or sell at a specific price. This can be useful when the trader is worried that a certain stock will decline or rise in value and would like to protect their investment.

In options, there is also a chance of making more money than what was initially invested. The price fluctuation of stocks has no limit and so does profit potential in options trading. The option is cheap enough so that if something goes right, there is still a large profit margin that can be achieved. After the expiration date, the seller of options can exercise his right to sell or buy the security at the specified level.

Chapter 4: Why is Options Trading Worth the Risk?

When stocks and bonds do just fine, there is always uncertainty about why traders prefer options. The huge gap in earnings potential is what others seem to miss out on. In general, stocks yield a profit of 8%–12% per year, which is very remarkable in and of itself. Nevertheless, alternatives are much more lucrative with much greater potential.

Usually, some option trades produce profits above 50%. It is not unheard of to make 100% gains in a short time and even more. This is why a lot of seasoned traders prefer alternatives. They are highly lucrative and immensely successful. In any market conditions, it is also possible to make money selling options. When the market is bullish, bearish, and even when it is sluggish, traders will make money. You do not need unique market conditions and profitability is therefore very feasible across the year.

Experts believe that trading options provide lots of advantages that other types of securities do not offer. Although not all traders may want to participate in trading options, other traders find it appealing in some ways.

Potential for Astronomical Profits

The prospect of making substantially significant profits relative to all other forms of trade in the markets is one of the key reasons for trading options. Also, without large amounts of capital, this is possible. Leverage is the concept behind this strategy. There is no need for a trader to have vast sums of money to gain big profits. For example, with as little as $10,000, simply using leverage, it is possible to gain sums such as $300,000 or even $800,000.

Take the example of a $10,000 trader whose trading fund. The trader needs to invest this amount in the ABC business. The current stock price is now $20, and it is anticipated that this price will increase. The trader could directly buy the shares using the funds and obtain 500 shares for his money. The trader would have made $5 per share, or a total of $2,500 in profits if the stock price were to rise to $25 within a month.

Alternatively, with the same amount of capital, the trader might buy call options for XYZ stocks. The options cause the investor, within a certain time, to buy back the underlying stocks. Option contracts now cost between $1 and $4, depending on some variables, such as the underlying security value. In our example, one call option costs $2, so the trader receives 5,000 option agreements for the $10,000.

In the next month, if the trader decides to exercise the right to sell the underlying stock, he stands to make a profit of $5 per share.

Note that, for a net profit of $25,000, he has a right to a total of 5,000 shares. This shows the potential and strength of alternatives and how successful this form of exchange can be.

Great Risk vs. Reward Consideration

Like all good traders, it is important to weigh the risk presented by a certain trade compared to the potential rewards. Then the style adapted would show the type of risk inherent in the trade when trading with options. The above example clearly illustrates how lucrative the trading process for options is. If a loss were to be sustained in the above case, then the total loss would have been the cost of the options.

In this case, since the amount set to be lost is negligible relative to the amount of profit to be made, the risk is well worth the reward. The higher the risk, in general, the higher the potential return. The risk versus reward ratio should be considered if a trader considers a deal.

You should learn how to gain from volatility as an options trader. As you may benefit from sharp and rapid changes in the markets, uncertainty must be your friend and partner. Options are primarily driven by implied volatility, which is the most significant factor influencing the price of options. You need to read and decide whether it is low or high to be on the lookout for implied volatility.

This way, you will quickly get a sense of direction about the sort of options in which to engage.

Versatility and Flexibility

The inherent versatility is another highly enticing advantage of investing in options. With hundreds of different tactics to try, choices offer plenty of versatility. This contrasts well with various other options for trade and investment out there. Many of these do not have as much versatility as alternatives do. There are also restricted strategies for most other securities, which tend to restrict a trader's versatility on that security.

Take stocks as an example. Also, stock traders face limitations, which are not inherent in the trading of options. Several methods vary from basic to intermediate to complex strategies. Stock traders purchase, retain, or sell stocks in general. Not much else is there that they can do. Because of the thousands of methods available to them, this compares considerably with alternatives. The versatility and flexibility inherent in the trading of options much exceed that of any other securities.

Firstly, the versatility of options enables them to be exchanged depending on a wide range of underlying securities. The variety and number of choices are immense. Besides, spreads have real versatility in the way they can be traded. There are many opportunities available for traders to have flexibility and agility in minimizing the risks of taking market positions when it comes to hedging and even simply attempting to profit from stock fluctuations.

Downsides of Options Trading

While the trading of options can be highly lucrative, it can also be extremely devastating. This is why beginners need to stick to the fundamental approaches before adequate information, understanding, and experience are acquired. It would be possible to implement more nuanced and even complex strategies after a while, which are very likely to profit irrespective of market conditions. However, risks exist, so it is always best to be careful at the outset.

Traders must consider the risks and drawbacks associated with options for trading. With the hope of cashing in on this lucrative trade, the various benefits have seen more and more traders, both amateurs and professionals, move into the world of options.

Not an Easy Task

It is advisable, first of all, to remember that trading options are not as easy as they look. The options are complicated bonds. They are agreements that come with certain conditions. It is important to grasp and consider these words at all times. Part of the contracts on options has to do with time. Options have a time limit, unlike stocks and other securities. They are extremely short-lived by this time decay factor. If a trading strategy doesn't work out, then worthless options will expire.

The dynamic existence is one of the most prohibitive considerations surrounding trading options. As they are difficult to master, countless traders avoid options. The fundamentals are pretty good and reasonably easy to understand. They have a limited range, however, as well as limited profitability. The compounded methods, which can be very difficult, lie in real profitability.

Traders will lose a lot of funds if they do not master options correctly. Since selling options are a complicated matter, it is also possible to lose more capital than invested. Therefore, trading can be an ominous and daunting assignment. More traders lose money than money is earned by those who do. An appreciation of the dynamic existence of choices is the biggest challenge. It is feasible to learn how to trade options, but it is a process that takes both effort and time. It can only be rewarded with success by traders who are committed and spend their time and effort.

Trading Options is a Risky Venture

The trading process for options is considered an extremely dangerous affair. A certain element of risk is present in all investment opportunities and even trading projects. Beginners and novices are the traders most at risk. Typically, these classes are not as well versed or adequately experienced to deal with alternatives.

In trading options, information is important, but experience is completely necessary. Instead of bleeding cash, traders tend to avoid trading options altogether.

Nevertheless, the trading method of options has been commonly used in risk management. To shield themselves from inherent losses, traders of shares and other securities sometimes purchase options. Let's say a trader holds ABC stock and expects its value to fall by 30% over the next month. In this event, this trader has two options. The first is selling the stock and expecting to get a great deal. As a way of hedging against any market risks, the other is to buy a call option.

A highly risky venture is selling options. And experienced traders lose money often. There are chances of making big profits, but there are also chances of losing substantial sums. It all relies on the tactics applied to the experience of a trader, and the sums involved. Trading stocks can be an incredibly dangerous undertaking, mostly for novice individuals.

The best advice is to read as much about trading options and grasp the fundamentals as easily as possible. Plenty of practice works as well. As much as possible, traders with little to no experience ought to put their expertise to use. There are plenty of websites that have dummy trading platforms where prospective traders can try various strategies.

There are also plenty of instruments and solutions that make it easier to exchange options. Both of these will result in better results in the markets when applied to various strategies. If the basic techniques are fully understood and mastered, a trader may continue to incorporate and finesse them until they are implemented flawlessly and confidently. This is how a trader moves from beginner to beginner, to intermediate, and finally skilled, trading levels.

The dynamic existence is one of the most prohibitive considerations surrounding trading options. As they are difficult to master, countless traders avoid options.

The compounded methods, which can be very difficult, lie in real profitability. This is why it can be very profitable to learn as much about options as possible. After taking months and often years to master them, many excellent traders have seen their fortunes turn around by simply applying these tactics.

Chapter 5: Trading Psychology

Many skills can help you be a successful trader in the world of options trading. It also consists of evaluating the company fundamentals and determining the direction of a stock trend. But, apart from all these, there is one more important skill. It is the psychology of the trader. Having emotion, thinking quickly, and exercising discipline are some of the main components of being collectively known as trading psychology. While talking about emotions, there are two types of emotions that you will need to keep under control—fear and greed.

Understanding Fear

Whenever a trader gets to know something bad about a stock or the entire economy, he/she will tend to feel scared. That is completely normal. The trader might start overreacting as well. He might think of liquidating all his holdings and sit on the cash. The trader might feel scared about making any other trade.

When you enter the world of trading, you are needed to have a clear understanding of what fear exactly is. It is a natural form of reaction that gets perceived to any kind of threat. In this case, the threat is meant for the potential nature of profits. When you start quantifying all your fears, it might help. You are required to find the root of your fear and find the reason behind it. But this form of thinking needs to appear before any bad news comes up and not after something bad has happened. When you think about it properly, by taking some time, you will learn how you perceive various small events. You will come to know the way you react to them. This will help you greatly to maintain a distance from your emotional responses. This whole thing might not feel that easy. But it is very important for the perfect health of your trading portfolio.

Opting or Research

You need to be an expert in the stocks and industries you find interest in. try your best to be updated with the market news, keep on educating yourself, and just keep your eyes open. If you get the opportunity of attending trading seminars, just go for them. You are required to dedicate most of your time to the research process. You will need to speak up with the trading management, study the data charts, read trading journals, and opt for background jobs such as industry analysis. As you continue studying and researching, you can gain more ideas about options trading. You can overcome the darkness of fear with this.

Speedy Decisions

Traders are required to think quickly and make super-fast decisions at times. You are being a trader and might need to sell out and buy stocks on a very short time notice. To accomplish all these, you will need to maintain a particular presence in your mind. You need to be disciplined to stick to your plans of action. You are required to know the perfect time for generating profits and incurring losses. There is no way in which you can permit your emotions to come in the way of decision-making.

Fighting Greed

'Pigs get slaughtered' is a very common saying on Wall Street. This indicates the traders' greedy habit of sticking to one position for winning for a very long time. It is done to get every penny from the rise of the stock price. The same stock will soon take a reverse turn, and you will get trapped as a greedy investor. Greed is not at all an easy thing to fight with. It is completely based on the instincts of human beings to do even better. It is the habit of gaining a little more than what you are currently having. It involves the sense of being unsatisfied. If you want to be successful in the world of trading, you will need to identify this instinct of yours. You will need to set a plan based on your rational way of thoughts, accompanied by no forms of whims or instincts.

Setting Rules

A trader must design new rules every day and follow them whenever the hit of psychology comes into the picture. You can start by setting out various guidelines based on your risk-award tolerance when you make any trade. You will need to ensure your profit target from a trade and employ stop loss for moving away from all your emotions from its way. You can also determine the types of events, positive or negative, that will be triggering the decisions related to selling or buying any stock. It would be good for you if you could just out certainly limit to the maximum amount that you will be profiting or losing in one day. After you have touched your decided mark, take out all your money, and just run. If a trade has already hit the loss target, it would be better for you to pack up your bags and return home.

Either of the two ways, you will be able to live for trading on the next day. If you try to move away from the limits, the time is near when you will be losing all you have, with no chance of trading soon. Trading is a risky affair, my friend. You need to look out for the perfect conditions and identify your limits to make the best out of you.

Being Flexible

You need to be flexible as being an investor. You will need to find out some time to experiment at fixed intervals. For example, you might think of investing in options to mitigate all your risks. The only way by which you can grab all the knowledge about the market of trading is by experimenting. The experience that you will be gaining from the events can assist you in controlling your emotions. You will need to assess your performance. As you evaluate your trading performances, it can help reflect how you have prepared yourself for the new trading session. You need to be updated about every condition of the market to modify your plans according to the condition. Being flexible is the key to successful trading as if you try to be confined within your fixed plans, you will lose chances. This is mainly because of the volatile nature of the trading market.

Chapter 6: Classic Mistakes to Avoid

Poor Speculation

The concept of speculation is that one is investing in stock in the hopes of it growing over time. Certain stocks are more "speculative." These are the stocks that the investor is not sure about. They may not be well-established but hold the potential for high growth. The investor will invest in these stocks hoping that they will generate a high return for them. Investors must develop their skills in picking the right stocks. They mustn't risk it all on stocks that perform poorly. For this reason, investors should familiarize themselves with how to speculate correctly.

Diversification Issues

It is falling in love with one company and failure to diversify. This mistake can take shape when we are talking about large, well-known companies. For example, as everyone knows, Apple has its so-called fanboys who love the company to the point of absurdity. It does have the right products that sell, of course, but when you love a company that much, it might cloud your investment decisions. Again, don't take it the wrong way—obviously, Apple has been a good investment decision for many people, so it worked out. But it won't always work out, and as they say, nothing lasts forever. While we're confident Apple will be around for a very long time, it may not be as dominant in the future as it has been the past decade. And that lack of dominance means its stock will become lackluster. Not a loser, for sure, but it is not going to skyrocket like it did after the iPhone was released.

Improper Education and Research

Not understanding the markets is the first mistake newbies often make. Before you get out your wallet or bank card, make sure that you know the basics before you start buying. That means having a good idea of what all the index funds mean, some basic stock market jargon, and knowing the different ways you can purchase stock. It's also essential to understand the markets on another level.

Not Having Clear Investment Goals

Investing is not a gambling casino; it's a place where you invest real money into real businesses. To achieve success, you need to have clear investment goals. This comes from two sides—the investment side and the end game side.

Next, you should have a clear idea of where you want to invest your money. Too many people just go around not thinking very far ahead and then hear about some hot new company "buy gold" or "invest in crypto" and then jump on the bandwagon. Impulse is not good to have as a part of your investment goal bag of goodies.

Once you've figured all this out, write down how you want to weigh each item. For example, suppose that Mary decides she wants to invest in the following areas:

- Healthcare,
- Technology,
- An index fund,
- Bonds

... but looking for high income.

The next thing Mary needs to do is think about what percentage of her investments she wants to devote to each of these four items. Since Mary is looking for high income from bonds, she probably wants to invest in some junk bonds that pay high-interest rates. Of course, "junk" bonds suggest they may default, so there is a bit of risk there. There is also some risk for technology stocks. These days, technology is changing rapidly, and today's giants might be knocked off the top by some currently unknown upstart. With that in mind, though Facebook or Apple might look secure now, you don't know if they will be secured and remain market leaders in ten years due to the sector itself being so volatile and ripe for disruption. Healthcare faces other issues. It might seem sensible to invest in large health insurance companies or health-related companies, but what if the public votes for politicians that want to install Medicare for all? That might diminish or even eliminate health insurance companies. On the other hand, if the current system stays mostly in place, then investments in big health-related companies like United Healthcare make good sense. So, Mary is taking a bit of a risk there too.

Since Mary has three risky investment choices, she decides to put 50% of her investments into an index fund, and she chooses an S&P 500 ETF. She then breaks up the other 50% by putting 10% into the bond investments, and then 20% each into technology and healthcare. Mary wants some security that comes with a fund like an S&P 500 ETF but also enjoys looking at individual stocks and doing her picking. Hence, she decides to buy stock in different companies for healthcare and technology.

The details of this little exercise aren't essential, and preferably, we simply want to illustrate how Mary has developed and executed a plan to organize her investments to get what she wants out of them. Now, she has to settle on a monetary figure that she will invest, and how often she will spend. Suppose that Mary plans to put $500 at the end of each month. Now Mary has planned her investment strategy, and as long as she sticks to her plan, she is likely to enjoy success.

Letting Emotions Rather Than Facts Govern Decisions

Emotions have a nasty way of injecting themselves into stock market investing. It's exciting and can be filled with fear if you're looking at losing your shirt. Of course, the real problem is that people overestimate the dangers. In particular, people have a short-term outlook. So, if they are in the midst of a crash as we were in 2008, people see the stock market dropping and think it's the end of the world. Going into a panic and wanting to sell before you think the market will bottom out is a naïve and emotionally based approach. Markets never bottom out and stay there.

A second area where emotions rear their ugly heads is in picking stocks. People often pick stocks using feelings rather than facts. That is not a way to generate long-term success in the markets.

Lack of Planning

The common mistake made by beginners is not planning their trades. To be an experienced trader, you need to work smart for it. You can't make up a mind map for how you think you can carry on the trade. Proper working and research are called for. You need to jot down the risks, the potential gains, and the cost to revenue ratio.

Without knowing your entry and exit points, and the amount of capital required to invest in the trade, you'll be lost, and guesswork leads to damages for anyone involved. Also, notice that straying from it can only make things worse once you make up a trading plan. If you stick to your well-formed plan, you will be successful.

Other Common Day Trading Mistakes and How to Avoid Them

Before you engage in the trade, here are some of the mistakes you need to beware of:

1. Adding more capital to a trade that is going.
2. Continuing to trade even after losing consecutively.
3. Not setting stop-loss parameters.
4. Working with the wrong broker.
5. Taking several related trades.
6. Investing in what you are not ready to lose.
7. Entering the trade blindly.
8. Not carrying out an analysis of the market.
9. Not having a plan.
10. Predicting news before it comes out.

Why and How Most Traders Fail

Trading in the stock market requires a combination of skills and experience to ensure that a trader can profit. An intraday trader also applies them to enable them to gain in a single day while simultaneously avoiding losses in the market. However, many traders seem to experience more losses than gains while trading in the short amount of intraday markets. These traders fail because they have weaknesses regarding their knowledge, skills, mindset, and trade expectations. Here are how these factors affect a trader and lead to his or her failure in the market.

Inadequate Knowledge

Knowledge is an essential tool to possess in any aspect of life. It is especially vital to a trader as it provides him or her with the expertise that develops and improves their trading skills. Thus, when a trader does not have adequate and proper education about trading, they set themselves up for a disastrous trading experience. He or she does not understand the trading tools and lacks the analytical thinking that forms the essence of trade. Consequently, they cannot make trading strategies or implement risk management rules, leading to losses and failure in the stock market.

Poor Skills

Some traders fail in the markets because they know how to achieve success, but they don't have the skills needed. A trader who does not continually practice his or her trading will result in having poor skills. Day trading is a business that requires a person to learn and train continuously for several years before he or she can identify as a proper trader. However, many traders have little training and experience in the markets and view themselves as qualified. It leads to the traders taking on more than they can handle, which ultimately leads to failure.

Mindset

The psychology of a trader can determine whether he or she succeeds in the trade. Most traders may fail in trading despite having adequate skills and experience due to psychological weaknesses. They approach the trades with the wrong emotions and attitudes that lead to unsuccessful ventures.

- Emotions – A trader lets his or her feelings influence their decisions and actions in the market. He or she allows his or her fear of losing money to control him or her. The trader ends up panicking and rushing into risky decisions that cause losses.
- Attitude – A trader has a flawed approach where he or she lets greed and overconfidence dictate their judgments. The trader thinks he or she is invincible and views the market as a playground. He or she takes risky positions that eventually lead to failure.

Unrealistic Expectations

Most traders think that they will succeed and leave no room for losses. Such a trader believes that their trading strategies are perfect, and they take trades with higher risks. He or she trades assuming in luck rather than the actual conditions of the market. As a result, they risk too much and apply poor trading strategies that backfire and lead to significant losses. Additionally, a trader's unrealistic expectation of profits leads to him or her being impatient and entering a trade with little training and planning. These factors combine to ensure the failure of a trader in the market.

Chapter 7: Common Pitfalls in Options Trading

All successful options traders go through a learning curve before they start profiting consistently. Some of them put in an all-out effort to learn by spending countless hours reading on the topic or watching video tutorials. Others learn at a more leisurely pace and once they get a grip of the basics, they lean more towards learning from their own experience.

Buying Naked Options Without Hedging

This is one of the most fundamental mistakes made by amateur options traders and is also one of the costliest ones that could make them go broke in no time.

Buying naked options means buying options without any protective trades to cover your investment if the underlying security moves against your expectations and hurts your trade.

For a person to make a profit after buying a naked option, the following things should fall in place:

- The trader should predict the direction of the underlying stock's movement correctly.

- The directional movement of the stock price should be quick enough so that the position can be closed before its gains get overrun by time-decay.
- The rise in the option's premium price should also compensate for any potential drop in implied volatility from when the option was purchased.
- The trader should exit the trade at the right time before a reversal of the stock movement happens.

It is impractical to expect everything to fall in place simultaneously always and that is why naked-options traders often end up losing money even when they correctly guess the direction of the underlying stock's movement.

Having said all this, many such traders often think they would fare better the ensuing time after a botched trade, rinse and repeat their actions till they reach a point where they would have lost most of their capital and are forced to quit trading altogether.

My advice to you—never buy naked options (unless it is part of a larger strategy to hedge some position) because it's simply not worth the risk.

Note: While buying naked-options has only finite risk limited to the price of the premium paid, selling of naked-options has unlimited risk and has to be avoided too unless hedged properly.

Underestimating Time-Decay

A second major mistake of inexperienced traders is underestimating time-decay.

Time-decay is your worst enemy if you are the buyer of an option and you don't get a chance to exit your trade quickly enough.

If you are a call options buyer, you will notice that sometimes even when your underlying stock's price increases every day, your call option's price still doesn't rise or even falls. Alternatively, if you are a put options buyer, you sometimes notice that your put option's price doesn't increase despite a fall in the underlying stock price. Both these situations can be confusing to somebody new to options trading.

The above problems occur when the rate of increase/decrease in the underlying stock's price is just not enough to outstrip the rate at which the option's time-value is eroding every day.

Therefore, any trading strategy deployed by an options trader should ideally have a method of countering/minimizing the effect of time-decay or should make time-decay work in its favor, to ensure a profitable trade.

Buying Options with High Implied Volatility

Buying options in times of high volatility is yet another common mistake.

During times of high volatility, option premiums can get ridiculously overpriced and at such times, if an options trader buys options, even if the stock moves sharply in line with the trader's expectation, a large drop in the implied volatility would result in the option prices falling by a fair amount, resulting in losses to the buyer.

A particular situation I remember happened the day the results of the "Brexit" referendum came through. The Nifty index reacting to the result (like most other global indices such as the Nasdaq 100) fell very sharply and the volatility index (VIX) jumped up by over 30%. The options premium for all Nifty options had become ludicrously high that day. However, this rise in volatility was only because of the market's knee-jerk reaction to an unexpected result. A couple of days earlier, the market stabilized and started rising again; the VIX fell sharply and brought down option premium prices accordingly.

Options traders who bought options at the time VIX was high would have realized their mistake a day or two earlier when the option prices came down causing them substantial losses because the volatility started to get back to normal figures.

Not Cutting Losses on Time

There is a famous saying among the folks on Wall Street—"Cut your losses short and let your winners run."

Even the most experienced options traders will make a bad trade once in a while. However, what differentiates them from a novice is knowing when to concede defeat and cut their losses. Amateurs hold on to losing trades in the hope they'll bounce back and eventually end up losing a larger chunk of their capital. The experienced traders, who know when to concede defeat, pull out early and re-invest the capital elsewhere.

Cutting losses in time is crucial especially when you trade a directional strategy and make a wrong call. The practical thing to do is to exit a losing position if it moves against expectation and erodes more than 2–3% of your total capital.

If you are a trader who strictly uses spread-based strategies, your losses will always be far more limited whenever you make a wrong call. Nevertheless, irrespective of the strategy used, when it becomes evident that the probability of profiting from trade is too less for whatsoever reason, it is prudent to cut losses and reinvest in a different position that has a greater chance of success rather than simply crossing your fingers or appealing to a higher power.

Don't Keep All Eggs in One Basket

The experienced hands always know that once in a while, they will lose the trade. They also know that they should never bet too much on a single trade which could considerably erode their capital were it to go wrong.

Professionals spread their risk across different trades and keep a maximum exposure of not more than 4–5% of their total available capital in a single trade for this very reason.

Therefore, if you have a total capital of $10,000, do not enter any single trade that has a risk of losing more than $500 in the worst-case scenario. Following such a practice will ensure the occasional loss is something you can absorb without seriously eroding your cash reserve. Fail to follow this rule and you may have the misfortune of seeing many months of profits wiped out by one losing trade.

Using Brokers Who Charge High Brokerages

A penny saved is a penny earned!

When I first entered the stock market many years ago, I didn't pay much attention to the brokerage I was paying. After all, the trading services I received were from one of the country's largest and most reputed banks. My provider's brokerage wasn't very different from that of other banks that provided similar services.

Many discount brokerage firms started flourishing that charge considerably less over the years, but I had not bothered changing my broker since I was used to the old one.

Only when I quantified the differences did I realize having a low-cost broker made a huge difference.

If you are somebody who trades in the Indian Stock markets, check the table below for a quantified break-up of how brokerage charges can eat into your earnings over a year if you choose the wrong broker. The regular broker in the table below is the bank whose trading services I had been hitherto using, and the discount broker is the one I use now. For the record, the former is also India's third-largest bank in the private sector, and the latter is the most respected discount broker house in the country.

Also, it is not just the brokerage that burns a hole in your pocket; the annual maintenance fee is also higher for a regular broker, and all these costs will make a huge difference in the long run.

Do a quantitative comparison using a table (something similar to the one I used above), and that would make it easier to decide who you should go with.

Note for India-based Traders: If you are a trader based in India or trade in the Indian Stock markets, I will strongly suggest using Zerodha, which has been consistently rated the best discount broker in the country.

Question and Answer

Give a Typical Example of Buying Naked Options Without Hedging?

A trader strongly feels a particular stock will go up in the short-term and assumes he can make a huge profit by buying a few call options and therefore goes ahead with the purchase. The trader knows if the underlying stock's price were to rise as expected, the potential upside on the profits would be unlimited, whereas, if it were to go down, the maximum loss would be curtailed to just the amount invested for purchasing the call options.

In theory, the trader's assumption is right, and it may so happen that this one particular trade may pay off. However, in reality, it is equally possible the stock would not move as per expectations or may even fall. If the latter happens, the call options' prices would start falling rapidly and may never recover, thereby causing major losses to that trader.

It is almost impossible to predict the short-term movement of stock accurately every time. The trader who consistently keeps buying naked options hoping to get lucky is far more likely to lose much more than what he/she gains in the long-term.

Chapter 8: How to Get Started in Options Trading

By becoming an option purchaser and an option author, Options Traders will benefit. The feature allows for future gains throughout all turbulent periods and once the business is calm or less turbulent. This is important since asset values such as securities, currency, and resources are still changing; an opportunity approach can reap its benefits, regardless of whether the market dynamics are there. Here, we will learn how to analyze your performance for better earning. We will also discover how to establish a mindset, design an action plan, and understand options trading.

Options arrangements and plans that utilize them have described benefit and deficit to determine what income you gain or lose. If you offer a choice, the cost of the amount paid is the maximum you can earn, although there is also an infinite downside opportunity. If you buy a choice, the benefit will be infinite, and the expense of the offer fee is the maximum you will risk. A person stands to benefit from various market environments, from bull versus bear to horizontal stocks, relying on the event apps used. Spreads in options aim to limit all future assets and liabilities.

Essentials of Viability of Options

When the corresponding commodity, let us assume an inventory, rises just above exercise price until expiration, a covered call holder aims to generate a profit. If the offer drops underneath the strike price prior to the expiry, a putting option generates a benefit. The precise amount of benefit depends on the discrepancy between all the value of the shares and the strike price of both the option at the termination or closing of the contract period.

If the fund manager remains underneath the strike point, a call option writer expects to make a return. The investor gains by writing a futures contract if the price remains above the discount rate. The productivity of a choice writer is restricted to the reward they earn for composing the alternative (which may be the expense of the model to estimate). Option authors are named dealers of alternatives, too.

Purchase vs. Writing Option

An option holder, when the option deal checks out, will make a considerable financial return. That's due to the price of a stock will move considerably above the market price. When the options exchange is lucrative, an options trader earns a relatively lower return. That's due to the returns of the author, no matter which way the stock travels, is restricted to the premium. How some write choices, then? Since the chances are generally on the choice writer's side disproportionately. Research showed that a few certain 75% of all expiry options expire without meaning. This analysis eliminates choice roles preceding to expiry that were marked out or practiced. Even then, there would be three out of OTM for every choice agreement, and ITM at termination or otherwise useless is a fairly revealing figure.

Analysis Yourself and Evaluate Performance

Analysis of Your Risk Tolerance

In order to decide if you are more of a model to estimate or even an option blogger, here's a quick test to measure your investment goals. Now let us assume that ten call option agreements can be bought or written, with each call's value at dollar 0.50. Generally, each agreement has 100 shares as the investment product, so $500 ($0.50 X 100 X 10 deals) will cost ten contracts.

You spend $500 if you acquire ten call option agreements, and it's the highest loss which you will suffer. Your future advantage, furthermore, is potentially unlimited. So, what is the trap, then? There is not a really large likelihood of the exchange becoming lucrative. While this chance depends on the volatility of both the call option implied as well as the period left to expire, let us just assume it is indeed 25%. On the other side, the gross advantage is the value of the premium revenue, or $500, whether you write ten call choice contracts, whereas the loss is potentially infinite. However, the chances of options trading being profitable are much more on your side, at 75%.

Will you gamble $500, thinking your 75% likely to lose your money and 25% likely to make a profit? Or perhaps you'd like to make a total of $500, recognizing that you should have a 75% probability of retaining the full sum or half of it because you have a 25% annual risk of winning the trade? The response to these questions would lead to an understanding of your investment behavior but whether you're best off becoming a buyer of options or an option editor.

It is vital to remember that those were the general figures common to all options, so becoming an alternative writer or perhaps a buyer in a particular commodity can be more valuable at some periods. Implementing the correct approach at the right moment could dramatically alter these changes.

Evaluating Your Performance

1. Risk/Reward

Although calls, as well as puts, could be assembled to produce complex choice strategies in different combinations, let's analyze the threat of the four simplest methods.

2. Buying a Call

This is the most fundamental path to choosing. As the overall cost is confined to the price charged for purchasing the call, whereas the maximum profit is theoretically unlimited, it is a reasonably low-risk approach. Although the chances of the exchange becoming quite lucrative are generally reasonably slim. 'Low risk' means that the overall expense of the option includes a very limited proportion of the wealth of the trader. It will make it a very dangerous trade to bet all resources on a sole call option since all the assets may be wasted unless the call expired worthlessly.

3. Buying a Put

This is just another reasonably low-risk tactic; however, if the trade turns out, that potentially huge profit. A feasible solution to the riskier option of shorting stocks the tradition offers is purchasing puts. Puts could also be acquired in a portfolio to hedge potential upside. The put purchaser's investment profile is somewhat less attractive than those of a cash flows are based, though, since equity indices usually grow higher over time, which implies that securities on average appear to advance more frequently than they fall.

4. Writing a Put

Put drafting is a favorite technique to professional market participants since the stock is allocated to the put author under the worst situation (they get to acquire the stock). In contrast, the perfect situation is where the writer keeps the entire sum of both the premium paid. The greatest danger in publishing is that, if it ultimately tanks, each writer can ultimately pay more than that for a stock. Although the overall benefit is equivalent to the premium paid, the risk/reward model of put composing is more negative than put or call purchasing, but the maximum loss is far greater. That can be said as the hope of being able to earn a profit is greater.

5. Writing a Call

Call writing available in 2 ways, bare and covered. The favored technique among moderate to experienced options traders has covered call writing, and it is commonly used to produce extra revenue from a fund. This because of calls on inventories kept inside the portfolio. The sole property of risk-tolerant, skilled retail investors is exposed or naked call reading since it has a risk profile close to a limited stock deal. In In-Call publishing, the overall incentive equals the premium paid. For a covered call approach, the greatest concern is that spending the rest would be "called away." The potential liability is potentially limitless for bare call writing, much like for a short sell.

6. Options Spreads

Using a spread tactic, traders or buyers sometimes merge stocks, purchasing one or more options to offer one or more other options. Propagation would cover the premium charged when the premium of choice offered is net against the premium of both the options bought. In addition, a spread's cost and benefit curves will cap the possible benefit or loss. To enjoy the benefits of the expected market action, you can generate stacks that can range from the basic to the complicated. Any spread technique may be either acquired or transferred, as with people options.

Mind Setup for Options Trading

The correct mentality is key to becoming a good trader. It operates on the minds of investors through the amygdala and hypnotherapy to combat's theory. Efficient investing requires personality manipulation in which the various feelings that come into influence eventually flounder on anyone that focuses solely on charts and patterns. It's a universal misconception of choices that are nuanced and dangerous. That being said, the fact would be that options are little more than a method to obtain leverage in numerous forms to stocks. Users see categorizing choices as difficult to comprehend as very straightforward, but having only a few simple choice characteristics allows them very beneficial and easily understood. Everyone can discover how and when to trade options with confidence by maintaining points in mind.

Options should also be considered as an expansion of stocks: What if you're in a role as a seller where you're not sure if you might keep a stock then let it go? Because when an investment has encountered setbacks, someone that has exchanged before has definitely experienced the problem and in cases, obtaining choices at your side makes for much-required stability.

Through stock trading only, you are restricted to initiating positive exposure through acquiring shares but bullish exposures by short-selling shares. Your path to a profitable trade resides in the tools to successfully guess the company's stock course, and while you can gamble long or short for less average danger and lower investment outlay for options. These extra advantages are only a small proportion of what is accessible when options are exchanged. However, the main message here seems to be that options were little more than additional options that investors have to convey an investing concept in their tool chest.

Choices will put the chances in your direction: Genuinely that trading options will enable you to position the chances in certain favor, implying you can position trades in which you have a good opportunity of being productive than 50%! As relative to equity trading alone, that those are not transactions that add additional risk. They will, in effect, help decrease your harm.

If you purchase a stock, you really need inventory to grow for all of you to prosper. You also want the inventory to go up for you all to win while you short-sell an inventory. These two trades explain results of 50% essentially, no particular edge. So, think you're optimistic about a company, and now if the stock increases, stays steady, or declines a tiny amount, you have the potential to earn profits. This is when options will become vital to a good portfolio.

Chapter 9: The Role of the Underlying Stock

It's vital to understand that stocks do play a fundamental role in options trading—even though they may not be what you are buying and selling. Bear in mind that an option is only a piece of paper that gives you the right to buy or sell a stock. Without the stock, you would have nothing to buy or sell.

You might say that the stock is Oz behind the curtain, changing and moving while your attention is fixed elsewhere. Letting Oz get up to his tricks without you is a bad idea. You need to be keeping an eye on your stocks just as much as you follow the options themselves.

Not every stock is allowed to have its options traded on an options exchange. In total, you'll find somewhere in the region of 3,600 stocks spread across twelve different exchanges, although that number changes all the time.

What does that mean? Well, the exchanges have some excellent rules that dictate which stocks may and may not participate in options trading. You'll find some of the biggest business names on the planet have options, and you'll also find what are known as "penny stocks," which buy and sell for less than $3.

In general, penny stocks will not be suitable for options trading. There simply isn't enough liquidity at such a small price for you to bother with the effort required to trade them.

Instead, I would recommend sticking with the big names—the recognizable companies such as Microsoft, Apple, Google, and McDonald's.

Another point to bear in mind is that there is a fixed relationship between options trading and the underlying stock. One option contract will always be equal to 100 stock shares.

In other words, a single contract will give you the right to buy or sell 100 shares of a stock. Multiply the number of contracts involved in a trade by 100 and you'll know how many shares are involved.

The third factor of that relationship between an option and its underlying stock is that whenever the stock goes up or down, in most cases so, too, will the option contract.

Because a stock and its options are so inextricably linked, you will need to study the stock market in detail to be a whiz at options trading. You will need to be able to predict which stocks are going to head in which direction and when—only if you get that right will your trading be truly successful.

For that reason, a lot of options traders started with the stock market, itself, and gave themselves the experience of the market's whims before taking a step up to the next level. If you haven't done that, it will be worth spending a month or more trading on the stock market. Even a theoretical portfolio that you manage and never pay a penny to invest in is a helpful step.

Doing that will allow you to get a sense of how the market functions overall and it will familiarize you with some of the stocks you might be interested in for trading with options. The best options traders have almost a sixth sense of how an underlying stock is going to perform. The only way to develop that uncanny ability is through exposure, research, and experience.

Chapter 10: Understanding the Strike Price

Strike Price

There is a fixed price that is a part of the contract for a call option, which allows the buyer to purchase any amount of stock corresponding to a specific company at a pre-determined. The set price contained in the contract can be termed as the "strike price". The strike price of this kind of contract is one of its most essential characteristics, and when you go to look for options to trade, you are going to see them listed in order by strike price. So, who do you purchase the shares from? You would buy the shares from the seller of the options contract. In the event they were not able to fulfill their end of the deal, the broker would step in and then do it for them (with consequences to the seller). The strike price must be used independently of the stock's current market valuation. As such, if there is a strike price of $50, but the stock's current market valuation has risen to $350 per share, it's not relevant. The seller of the call option would still be required by law to sell you 100 shares at $50 a share.

The concept doesn't change for put options. In this case, this kind of contract's strike price entitles the holder to trade a specific amount of stock. As in the case of call options, you would be selling the shares to the originator of the put option. They would be legally bound to buy the shares of the stock whose valuation has been determined by the seller regardless of its perceived current market valuation.

Expiration Date

Next, we come to the other crucial piece of information, which is the date of the expiration date of the contract itself. When you select a given expiration date, you will then see options listed by strike price. On some platforms, options are all listed on the same page but grouped according to type. So, you will see all the call options listed at the top, and then this will be followed by the put options. In other cases, you will see a tab that lets you move back and forth between call and put options for the same expiration date.

As we will see, the expiration date is very important for many reasons. As this critical deadline approaches, if the contract does not have an appropriate valuation with regard to the stock's current market valuation, it's going to lose value rapidly. Let's get some insight into this with this sample situation. Let's assume that you are looking to purchase a contract for a call option that has a current strike valuation of $10. With this trade, you are looking to make a profit when its price increases. As such, the option has the greatest value when its current market valuation exceeds $10. Consequently, you profit more, the higher the price gets. Now, let's assume that its current market valuation falls to $7 instead. Then that call option simply isn't worth anything. People can just buy shares for $7, so why would anyone enter into a contract that required them to buy shares at $10 a share? Of course, they wouldn't do that. The longer you have remaining in the deal, the greater the value. If there are three months left on the contract, then it might still have a little value, because there would be a chance that the stock could move significantly in that time frame. But, if there are only three days left on the contract, the chances of the stock increasing from $7 to above $10 are pretty much nil (unless an earnings call is coming up and it turns out to be unexpectedly rosy), so the option will be rapidly losing value.

The expiration date is also important because it may be in a position where it can be exercised when an option expires. Of course, there are as many approaches to this situation as there are unique individuals. Some people are small traders and simply don't want to buy or sell the stock, and they may not have the capital to do so even if they wanted to. Remember, we are talking about 100 shares for each option contract.

On the other hand, others may be looking to buy and sell the shares. So, they may want to exercise the option when it expires, or even beforehand. If you cannot buy and sell shares, you'll probably want to get out of the option before it expires to avoid this situation. In other words, you'll want to get whatever profits you can from selling the option. So, you want to sell it prior to the expiration date.

Chapter 11: Basic and Advance Trading – Selling Covered Calls

A covered call alludes to exchange in the money-related market in which the financial specialist selling call choices possesses the identical measure of fundamental security. To execute this, a speculator holding a long situation in advantage at that point composes (sells) call choices on that equivalent resource for creating a salary stream. The financial specialist's long situation in the advantage is the "spread" since it implies the merchant can convey the offers if the purchaser of the call alternative decides to work out. On the off chance that the financial specialist at the same time purchases stock and composes call alternatives against that stock position, it is known as a "purchase express" exchange.

Note:

- A secured call is a mainstream alternative methodology used to create pay-as-choices premiums.
- To execute a secured call, a financial specialist holding a long situation in a benefit at that point composes (sells) call choices on that equivalent resource.

- It is regularly utilized by the individuals who mean to hold the fundamental stock for quite a while yet don't expect an obvious cost increment in the close to term.
- This methodology is perfect for a financial specialist who accepts the fundamental cost won't move a lot over the close term.

Understanding Covered Calls

Secured calls are an unbiased system, which means the financial specialist just anticipates a minor increment or reduction in the basic stock cost for the life of the composed call choice. This methodology is frequently utilized when a financial specialist has a transient unbiased view on the advantage and thus holds the benefit long and, at the same time, has a short position using the choice to produce salary from the choice premium.

If a specialist financial plans to hold the fundamental stock for quite a while yet doesn't expect a predictable cost increment in the close to term, then they can create salary (premiums) for their record. At the same time, they hold up out the break.

A secured call fills in as momentary support on a long stock position and permits financial specialists to acquire pay through the premium got for composing the choice. Nonetheless, the financial specialist relinquishes stock increases if the cost moves over the choice's strike cost. They are likewise committed to giving 100 offers at the strike cost (for each agreement composed) if the purchaser decides to practice the choice.

A secured call methodology isn't valuable for a bullish nor an exceptionally bearish speculator. If a financial specialist is exceptionally bullish, they are ordinarily happier, not composing the choice and simply holding the stock. The alternative tops the benefit on the stock, which could lessen the general benefit of the exchange if the stock value spikes. Correspondingly, if a speculator is extremely bearish, they might be in an ideal situation just selling the stock, since the premium got for composing a call alternative will do little to balance the misfortune on the stock if the stock falls.

Most Extreme Profit and Loss

The most extreme benefit of a secured call is identical to the strike cost of the short call choice, less the price tag of the basic stock, in addition to the premium got.

The greatest misfortune is proportionate to the price tag of the fundamental stock less the premium got.

Secured Call Example

A financial specialist claims portions of theoretical organization TSJ. They like its drawn-out possibilities just as its offer cost; however, they feel that in the shortest term, the stock will probably exchange general level, maybe inside two or three dollars of its present cost of $25.

If they sell a call alternative on TSJ with a strike cost of $27, they procure the premium from the choice deal be that as it may, for the span of the choice, top their upside on the stock to $27. Accept the top-notch they get for composing a three-month call choice is $0.75 ($75 per agreement or 100 offers).

One of two situations will play out

TSJ shares exchange beneath the $27 strike cost. The alternative will lapse useless, and the speculator will keep the premium from the choice. For this situation, by utilizing the purchase compose methodology, they have effectively beaten the stock. They despise everything; they own the stock but have $75 extra in their pocket, fewer expenses.

TSJ shares ascend above $27. The choice is worked out, and the upside in the stock is topped at $27. On the off chance that the cost goes above $27.75 (strike cost in addition to premium), the speculator would have been exceptional off holding the stock. Even though, on the off chance that they intended to sell at $27 in any case, composing the call alternative gave them an extra $0.75 per share.

Chapter 12: Benefits and Risks of Covered Calls

We, as a whole, realize that there is cash to be made by composing secured calls. You can generally discover the individuals who will swear that it is the best procedure that exists. And afterward, other people won't go anywhere near a secured call! Likewise, with any venture, there is dangers and advantages partner with exchanging secured calls too.

Because another person has had accomplishment with a specific method for contributing doesn't imply that it is an assurance of benefits for you. On the other hand, if you run over somebody who won't consider selling consider alternatives, it's not a sign that you should avoid that methodology.

There are advantages and dangers included when choosing to sell secured calls. It doesn't imply that you shouldn't contribute that way. It just implies that you should know about the advantages and disadvantages before you choose to sell your first-choice contract.

So, since nobody likes to hear awful news, we should talk about the advantages to your portfolio should you choose to compose approaches stocks that you own.

Pros

Composing secured calls can permit you to include an additional payment each month. By selling a secured approach shares that you are simply holding in your portfolio, you can produce an extra income stream over your profits and stock appreciation. Numerous individuals simply hold a stock for the profits; however, why not make additional benefits from secured call selling too! By realizing when to sell call choices (and if/when you have to repurchase them), you can quicken the rate at which your stock record develops in esteem.

Secured call composing allows you to profit from a stock that is inclining sideways. If you are likely to sell a stock once it has risen a couple of dollars, you can, in some cases, be disappointed when one of your properties just moves around a similar value you initially paid for it. Secured calls can give you an additional income while you are trusting that your stock will ascend in cost.

Selling call choices gives you multiple times the gaining power. A stock that has alternatives permits the proprietor to rehash the secured bring methodology again and again, after a seemingly endless amount of time after month, throughout the entire year. For the individuals who might not have any desire to watch their stock value changes each moment of the day, utilizing the secured call methodology liberates you to just make 12 exchanges for each year.

The excellent you gather from selling the call option(s) is all yours, regardless. Regardless of whether you are not gotten out at termination, you, despite everything, clutch the money you got from opening the position. You likewise don't need to sell the stock on the off chance that it doesn't close over the strike value you sold the choices at.

A regularly disregarded advantage to selling a secured call is that it can bring down the expense of purchasing portions of stock. On the off chance that you purchase stock and simultaneously sell your secured call, this is what's known as a purchase compose. If you somehow managed to purchase stock and afterward sell secured calls at a later point in time that would simply be selling a secured call.

Suppose that you needed to buy portions of stock that were as of now exchanging at $30 per share. The $30 call choice for that stock is estimated at $1.00. If you somehow managed to purchase the stock and sell the call alternatives, purchasing the stock would just cost you $29 per share ($30 for the stock less the $1 you get for selling the call choice). Indeed, even just offer secured calls to buy stock, still significantly brings down your expense for each position.

Cons

Selling call alternatives against your stock naturally tops your benefit potential should your stock pointedly ascend in esteem. If you sell a secured call at the $20 strike value, you pass up any benefit if the stock closes above $20 on termination. This is possibly the greatest disadvantage of the secured call system.

Opening a secured call placing doesn't shield you from having misfortunes either. It does anyway assist with securing your drawback hazard. You equal the initial investment moment that composing a call is the measure of the call alternative you sold deducted from the stock you paid for each offer. In our preceding model, we purchased stock at $30 per share. At that point, we sold calls that were $1.00 each. Our make back the initial investment in this situation would be $29. Should the stock close underneath $29 at termination, we would endure a misfortune in this position.

Should the stock drop and you need to offer your situation to forestall further misfortunes, you would need to repurchase your call choices before you can sell any of the offers. Repurchasing the call alternatives can likewise make further misfortunes in your portfolio.

To put it plainly, secured calls can be a beneficial methodology if you know about the dangers in question. Remember, there is no hazard-free approach to put resources into stocks other than never to purchase any. You benefit from your capacity to oversee chance, not by maintaining a strategic distance from it.

Risk of Covered Calls

Call vendors need to clutch basic offers or agreements, or they'll be holding exposed calls, which have hypothetically boundless misfortune potential if the basic security rises. Subsequently, merchants need to repurchase choice positions before termination if they need to sell offers or agreements, expanding exchange costs while bringing down net gains or expanding overall deficits.

Chapter 13: Outcomes of a Covered Call Sell

Covered calls are a well-liked type of call option strategy that is made when the investor only expects a little increase or decrease in the underlying asset's cost. These particular calls generate income through premiums, which are the costs that people pay to get the options.

The advantage of a covered call is that the investor gets into the option to carry a long position with the underlying asset. This way, they experience downside protection while earning passive income for the individual invested in this particular stock.

The big difference here is that a daily call option is taken for the short-term position, whereas a covered call option is taken for the long-term position. In the end, the covered call provides higher risk protection and greater earning potential.

How Does One Sell Covered Calls?

Selling covered calls mean that you get paid in exchange for giving up some of your future upsides. You generally do that as a way to ensure a rise in your prices while also creating passive income directly through selling the call option itself.

You engage in covered calls once you think that stock you have already purchased goes to increase in value over a long time. For instance, let's say you purchase ABC stock for $100 per share, and you think it will rise to $120 per share in 12 months. You might create a covered call option that permits people to buy the right to get that stock at $110 per share in six months, thus earning you the income from the contract's value, referred to as the premium, directly.

Then, if the buyers of your contract prefer to purchase the stock in six months, you furthermore may gain the profits from that sale. Although the profits might not be as large had you held the position for the whole six months, they are more guaranteed and reliable than earnings in the traditional open market.

Writing your covered call takes some practice, but it can earn you a huge amount of profit at the end of the day. The first thing you need to do is start with identifying what stock you already own in your portfolio that has been performing well, which you are prepared to sell if the call option is assigned to a buyer who wishes to exercise their right to buy.

Suppose you are bullish on a particular stock in the future. In that case, otherwise, you believe it will increase exponentially, avoid choosing that stock as you may not earn the maximum amount of profit through the covered call option. Instead, you would like to settle on a stock that you think goes to increase steadily, but not too incredibly high values so that you do not feel too heartbroken when it is time for you to spare that stock.

After you have chosen your stock, you are going to choose your strike price and your expiration date, which may, in turn, create your premium. These are the three elements of the contract that will outline how the buying and selling of your stock will work, what level of profit you will gain, and when that specific trade must be executed by so as for it to be valid.

Your strike price is the price that you feel you'd be comfortable selling your stock at. Once you are writing a covered call, you need to write down a strike price out of the money or less than the stock's present value. This way, if your buyer should prefer to enact their right to buy your stocks, you are earning profits. You need the stock value to increase before you have to sell it to ensure that you are set out to receive profits; otherwise, you may not receive any earnings from your trade deal.

The best way to pick your strike price is to look at how the stock has been performing thus far and how it is expected to perform going forward. You may want to conduct a technical analysis to make sure that you follow a trend that gives the most likely increase value for your stock prices. This way, once you set the strike price, you are remaining reasonable while also creating a profitable price point for yourself.

After you have picked your strike price, you need to call when the option goes to expire. Generally, call options expire within 30-45 days of their creation; however, you can certainly increase or decrease that length of time. You will want to pick an expiration date that permits you to shut out the trade quickly while also having a suitable premium that people are going to be willing to pay. If your expiration date turns the premium into a too high number, you may have difficulty selling your option; otherwise, you may never sell it at all.

After you create your strike price and expiry date, your premium will be automatically determined for your covered call option. Generally, investors will favor premiums of about 2% of the entire stock value, which ensures that they even have the chance to make the most off the trade while incurring the least number of losses.

This fact means that if you set your expiry date too far out in the future, you would possibly increase your premium's value too high, preventing investors from being eager to purchase it.

With that being said, always confirm that you are researching what has gone into creating your premium. Sometimes, premiums will seem abnormally high, which may occur if something is happening within the economy that may directly impact the stock price you are trading. If this happens, you will possibly get to adjust your covered call option or choose a particular underlying asset to trade.

Generally, if something seems too good to be accurate within the stock market, it is, so watch out for premiums that appear too high.

Outcomes of a Covered Call Sell

There are three possible outcomes that you could experience if you were to interact in a covered call sale. The first would occur if the stock price went down, the second would happen if the stock price stayed the same or slightly increased without reaching the strike price, and the third would occur if the stock rises past the strike price.

Each of those outcomes will have different results, and you would like to remember what might happen in each scenario:

- Outcome One: The Stock Rises Past the Strike Price

This scene takes place if the stock price rises above the strike price, which suggests that the decision option will be assigned, and you will be required to sell 100 shares of the stock to the buyer.

In this case, you may experience frustration for setting the strike price lower and not receiving the stock's total value to sell it. While you can still receive profits, they will not be as massive as they could have been, which is frustrating.

Still, you have made profits, so there is no reason to worry. You have earned more funds to place into your future trades, allowing you to increase your profitability with trading options.

- Outcome Two: The Stock Stays The same or Slightly Increases without Reaching the Strike Price

The second scenario is that the stock price barely fluctuates and never reaches the strike price. In this case, there is no bad news. The call option will expire worthlessly, and you can profit on the whole premium from selling it. You may also see some increase in your stock's value overall, adding a little more profit into your portfolio.

- Outcome Three: The Stock Price Goes Down

If the stock price were to go down at the option expiring time, the option would likely expire worthlessly. If the buyer were to exercise their right to buy, they might be paying above the stock price, which might not add up on their behalf. In this case, you'd keep the whole premium for selling the contract. The stock price would be down, which can be unfortunate for the rest of your portfolio, but it might be positive that you had profited from the cost of the premium.

If this happens, it is crucial to recollect that you are not locked into your contract position. The price of the call option you sold will also decrease in value, which suggests that you can purchase back the contract for less money than you sold it for that you aren't required to make the sale. Then, you can create a technique for a way you are going to manage the stock you have in your portfolio.

If you think that it will start moving out of favor, you can always dump it, or you can keep it and maintain your position if you feel that it is still going to behave as you anticipated it might be when you bought it in the first place.

Chapter 14: Stepping Up a Tier: Buying Calls

Buying calls is a more advanced form of training than selling covered calls. But it's not that complicated, so let's dive in.

What You're Actually Buying

Remember that one option contract is for 100 shares, so you'll need to be able to buy 100 shares of the stock in order to exercise your right to buy.

Also, remember that an options contract has a deadline. If the stock price fails to exceed the strike price by the deadline, you're out of luck and will lose whatever money that you invested in the premium. In relative terms, the premium price will be small, so chances are if you are careful and not starting out by buying large numbers of options contracts, you won't be out that much money.

Your Goal Buying Options Contracts

The goal when purchasing options contracts is to buy a stock at a price that is lower than its current market value. In other words, you want the stock price to be significantly higher than the strike price so that you're enjoying significant savings in purchasing the stock. When evaluating your options, you'll need to consider the added costs of the premium paid plus commissions. In some cases, commissions can be substantial, so make sure you know what they are ahead of time so that you choose a good strike price and exercise your options at the right time.

You're a Trader, Not an Investor

You may be mentally conditioned to think in terms of investing. An investor wants to build a diversified portfolio over a long time period that they believe will increase in value over the long term. Traders operate in the same way but have different objectives. They are looking for short-term profits, not investments because they will not hold these stocks. If you were interested in holding the stock, you would simply buy it at the lower price that is currently on offer. Your goal is to be able to buy at the strike price when the stock has increased significantly in price and then sell it immediately so that you can pocket the profits.

Let's take an example. Suppose that XYZ Corporation is currently selling at $30 a share. People are expecting the stock to rise, and some people are really bullish about its short-term prospects. If you are an investor, your goal is to get the stock at the lowest possible price and then hold it long-term. If you are using strategies like dollar-cost averaging, you might be buying a few shares every month without paying too much attention to what the price is specifically on the day you purchase. In any case, as an investor, you'll simply buy the shares at $30.

As a trader, you're hoping to cash in on the moves of XYZ over the next couple of months. You'll buy an options contract; let's say its premium is $0.90 and the strike price is $35. Your cost for the 100 shares is $90.

Then the stock price shoots up to $45. Since it passed the strike price, you can exercise your option to buy the shares at the strike price. You can buy them at $35 for a total price of $3,500. But remember—you're not an investor in for the long haul. You'll immediately unload the shares. You sell the shares for $4,500 and make a $1,000 profit. After considering your premium, your profit is $910. It will go a little bit lower after considering commissions, but you get the idea. The purpose of buying call options is to make fast profits on stocks you think are going to spike.

It's hard to guess when the best time is to really buy call options. Obviously, you don't want to do it when a major recession hit. The optimal time is during a bull market, or when a specific company is expected to hit on something big that will suddenly increase its value in the markets. A good time to look is also when a recession hits, but it passes the bottom out period.

Benefits of Buying Call Options

Call options have many benefits that we've already touched on earlier. In Particular:

- Call options allow you to control 100 shares of stock without actually investing in the 100 shares—unless they reach a price where you get the profit that you want.
- Call options allow you to sit and wait, patiently watching the market before making your move.
- If your bet doesn't work out, you're only going to lose a small amount of money on the contract. In our example, if XYZ loses value, and ends up at $28 per share instead of moving past your strike price of $35, then you're only out the $90 you paid for the premium.
- Call buying provides a way to leverage expensive stock.

What to Look for When Buying Call Options

Now let's take a look at some factors that you'll be on the lookout for when buying call options. You're going to want to be able to purchase shares of the stock you're interested in at a price that is less than the price you think it will go up to. You need to do this in order to ensure that the stock price surpasses the strike price. Of course, it's impossible to know what the future holds, so this will involve a bit of speculation. You'll have to do a lot of reading and research to make educated guesses on where you expect the stock to go in the next few weeks or months.

Second, you'll need to consider the cost of the premium when making your estimates. For the sake of simplicity, suppose that you find a call option with a premium of $1 per share. You're going to need a strike price that is high enough to take that into account. If you go for a stock that is $40 a share with a $1 premium and a strike price of $41, obviously, you're not going to make anything unless the stock price goes higher than $41.

Remember that exercising your rights on the options contract is not a path toward immediate money. You're going to have to turn around and sell it ASAP in order to profit. Of course, when you sell is a judgment call, as is when you exercise your right to buy. You're going to want to wait until the right moment to buy, but it's impossible to really know what that right moment is. This is where trading experience helps and even then, the most skilled experts can make mistakes. For a beginner, the best thing to do is exercise your right to buy the shares and then sell them as soon as they've gone far enough past the strike price for you to make a profit and cover the premium. If you wait too long, there is always the chance that the stock price will start declining again, and it will go below your strike price and never exceed it again before the contract expires.

Open Interest

If you get online to check stocks you're interested in, one of the measures you will see is "Open Interest." This tells you the number of open or outstanding derivative contracts there are for that particular stock. Every time that a buyer and seller enter into an options contract, this value increases by one. What you want to do with open interest as a trader looking to make real cash from call options is to look for stocks that show big movement in the number of open trades. You're going to want to look for increasing numbers. This means that other traders have an interest in buying call options on this stock and that they're expecting it to go up in value in the near future.

Of course, you're going to want to take an educated approach to this. Simply getting online and going through random stocks will be a waste of time, it might take you weeks to find something.

You're going to want to prepare ahead of time by keeping an eye on the financial news. Watch Fox Business, read the Wall Street Journal, and watch CNBC and read any other financial publications that are to your liking. Find out what stocks the experts are talking about and which ones they expect to make significant moves over the next few weeks and months. Keep in mind these people and experts often make mistakes, so you're only using it as a guideline. You also don't want to focus solely on looking for stocks that are going to make moves; you want to keep up with company news. You need to keep your ears open for news such as the development of a new drug or the latest electronic gadget. Sometimes you might find out news about that before the stock begins attracting a lot of interest in the markets.

Chapter 15: Strategies for Buying Calls

Tips for Buying Call Options

- Do not buy a call option with a strike price that you do not think the stock can beat.
- Always include the premium price in your analysis.
- Look for calls that are just in the money. These are likely to bring a modest profit.
- Call options that are out of the money might give you an opportunity for a cheaper premium.
- However, the premium should not be your primary consideration when looking to buy a call option. Compared to the money required to purchase the shares and the potential profits if the stock goes past the strike price, the premium is going to be a little cost in most cases—provided, of course, the strike price is high enough to take the rebate into account.
- Look at the time value. If you are looking for more substantial profits, it is better to aim for more extended contracts. Remember that with any call option you have the opportunity to buy the stock at the strike price at any time between today's date and the deadline when the stock market price exceeds the strike price. More extended time frames mean you increase the chances of that happening.

Even if the price goes a little above the strike price and dips down, with a longer window of time before the deadline, you can wait and see if it rebounds. Remember, if it never does, you are only out the premium.

- Start small. Beginning traders should not bet the farm on options. You will end up broke if you do that. The better approach is to start by investing in one contract at a time and gaining experience as you go.
- The best-case scenario for you, as the buyer, is that the stock suddenly starts rising at high speed before the deadline arrives. You want it to go beyond the strike price so that, when it comes time to exercise your right, you are purchasing your stock at a lower rate than it is now worth. Obviously, you then have the option to instantly list that stock as a covered sell, which would allow you to realize that profit in real money.
- That final piece of the puzzle is the important one. As an options trader, you are not in the business of building a stock portfolio. You do not really want to own those shares – you want to make a profit on them as they pass through your hands. You want to buy them for less than they are worth and then sell them on, perhaps even for more than they are worth if you are lucky. It is within that transaction your money will be made.

Buying calls has several advantages for you as an options trader:

- It does not cost much to get involved in the movement of a stock. You only need to fork out the amount for the premium, after which you can sit back and wait to see what the stock does before making your purchase decision based on actual information, rather than on speculating what the market will do.

- It allows you to make use of the kinds of "tips" that market experts have a terrible habit of swearing by. You read the news, watch the markets, and have information that makes you think an individual stock is about to rise fast and hard. Obviously, you want to take advantage of that, and options trading allows you to do so much more safely than merely buying the stock. If you are wrong, you will only lose your premium and you may even make a small profit. If you were wrong and purchased the stock and then it plummeted rather than rose, you stand to lose a whole lot more cash.

Chapter 16: Understanding Volatility

There's one final factor that affects the prices of contracts on a fundamental basis, though it's not something we've touched on so far. However, the volatility of a contract is an incredibly important concept to grasp for an options trader.

What is Volatility?

Volatility refers to the movement of the underlying stock. Some stocks will slowly wend their way up and down in a predictable manner—those are not very volatile. Others charge on a day-to-day basis and change between up and down along the way.

To sum up the effect of volatility in a single sentence: the more volatile the stock, the more that an options trader is willing to pay for it. A volatile stock has a better chance of reaching the strike price and perhaps shooting far beyond it before the expiration date.

However, it's also the most dangerous of the factors that you need to bear in mind because it's arguably the most likely one to force you into a bad decision. A volatile stock, for example, can lead to a much higher premium and therefore a higher contract price; unless that stock shoots through the roof, you could end up losing money even when you should be making it.

One way to estimate a stock's volatility is to take a look at what it has done in the recent past. This tells you how much it has moved up and down already, which some use as an indicator of how much it will move up and down in the future.

Unfortunately, it's not always true that the past repeats itself, and you can't predict the future based on what's already happened. Instead, options traders use "implied volatility" to make their guesses: the value that the market believes the option is worth.

You can see this reflected in the activity on the options for that stock. Buyers will be keen to get their hands-on options before a certain event takes place, such as the announcement of a new product or a release about the company's earnings. Because of this, options increase in price because there is implied volatility—the market thinks the stock is going to shoot up.

You'll see lower demand on a stock that's flat or moving gently because there is no implied volatility and, therefore no hurry to get in on the action. You'll also see correspondingly low prices for the option.

Volatility is a good thing—as a buyer, you want the stock to be volatile because you need it to climb to the strike price and beyond. However, there is also such a thing as too much volatility. This is when contracts become popular, prices rise up, and you stand to pay more for a contract than you will eventually earn.

Your brokers will likely be able to provide you with a program that will help you determine implied volatility, asking you to enter certain factors and then calculating it for you. However, it's only through experience that you'll learn how to spot a stock that's just volatile enough to justify its higher price—again, practice is the key.

It's also worth noting that a lot of the risk in options trading comes from volatility, largely because it's impossible to be accurate in your estimates. What happens if an earthquake destroys that company's headquarters? Stocks are going to plummet, and you had absolutely no way to see it coming.

That's why options traders are forced to accept that their fancy formulas are not going to be perfect predictors. They will help, but you should still be conservative in your trading and avoid the temptation to sink everything into a trade you believe could make your fortune thanks to its volatility.

Strategies for a Volatile Market

- Long Straddle

This strategy is essentially an amalgamation of the long call and long put trading strategies. You will be using the money options for executing the strategy. You are required to purchase at the money calls along with at the money puts of the same amount. Execute both these transactions simultaneously and ensure that the expiry date for them stays the same. Given that the expiry date is long-term, it gives the underlying security sufficient time to show a price movement and increases your chances of earning a profit. A short-term expiration date doesn't provide much scope for any changes in the price of an asset, so the profitability is also relatively low.

- Long Strangle

This is also known as the strangle strategy, and you must place simultaneous orders with your broker. You must purchase calls on relevant security and then by the same number of puts on the security. The options contracts you execute must be out of the money and must be made simultaneously. The best way to go about it is to purchase those securities that are just out of the money instead of ones that are far out of the money. Make sure that the strike prices in both these transactions are equidistant from the existing trading price of the underlying asset.

- Strip Straddle

This strategy is quite similar to a long straddle- you will be purchasing at the money calls and the money puts. The only difference is that the number of puts you purchase will be higher than the calls your purchase. The expiry date and the underlying asset for both these transactions you make will be the same. The only factor upon which your profitability lies is in the ratio of puts to calls you use. The best ratio is to purchase two puts for every call you make.

- Strip Strangle

You stand to earn a profit if the underlying asset makes a big price movement in either direction is. However, your profitability increases if the price movement is downwards instead of upwards. You will be required to purchase out of the money calls and out of the money puts. Ensure that the number of money puts you make are greater than the out of the money calls you to decide to make. So, to begin with, the ratio of 2:1 will work well for you.

- Strap Straddle

This is quite similar to the long straddle strategy- you are required to purchase at the money calls along with at the money puts for the same date of expiry. You are required to purchase more calls than ports, and the basic ratio to start with is 2:1. User strategy with certainty that there will be an upward movement in the underlying asset price rather than a downward price movement.

- Strap Strangle

This is quite similar to the Long strangle strategy and uses it when you're quite confident that there will be a dramatic movement in the price of the underlying strategy. You tend to earn a profit if the price moves in either direction, but your profitability increases in the price movement are upward. There are two transactions you must execute—purchase out of the money puts and purchase out of the money calls options. However, the number of out-of-the-money calls you to make must be greater than the out-of-the-money puts. The ratio of out of the money puts out-of-the-money calls must be two to one. So, you will essentially be purchasing twice as many calls as sports.

- Long Gut

You are required to purchase in-the-money call options along with an equal number of in-the-money put options. All of these will be based on the same underlying security along with the same date of expiration. The decisions you are required to make while using the strategy are related to the strike price you want to use and the date of expiration. It is suggested that to increase your profitability and reduce the upfront costs, the strike price you must opt for must be closely related to the current trading price of the underlying asset.

- Call Ratio Back Spread

You are required to purchase calls and the right calls to create a call ratio back spread. Since it is a ratio spread, the number of options you execute in each of these transactions will not be the same. As a rule of thumb, try to purchase two calls for every call you write. Always ensure that the total credit for the contracts you've written must be higher than the total debit for the contracts you have acquired.

- Put Ratio Back Spread

You will earn a profit if the price of the underlying asset moves in either direction; however, your profitability increases if the price of the underlying asset price goes down instead of going up. You are required to purchase puts and write puts simultaneously. As is obvious, both of these transactions will be based on the same underlying asset. The only difference is that instead of purchasing an equal number of puts, you will be purchasing to puts for every put you right. The puts you purchase must be at the money while the ones you write must be in the money. The expiry date, along with the underlying security, must be the same.

- Short Calendar Call Spread

The strategy is best used when you are certain that there will be a significant price movement in the value of the underlying security. However, you are uncertain of the direction in which the security will swing. Instead of spending a lot of time trying to analyze the direction of the price change, you can use the strategy. The strategy is likely complicated, and beginners must not attempt it on the first try. There are two transactions you must make.

The first transaction is to purchase at the money calls, and the second transaction is to write at the money calls. Since it is a calendar spread, the expiry date is used for both these transactions must be different. The options you decide to purchase must be short-term with a relatively close expiry date while the options you write must be long-term with a longer date of expiration.

- Short Calendar Put Spread

Two transactions are required to execute this strategy- purchase at the money puts while writing at the money puts. The date of expiration for both these transactions will be different since it is a calendar spread. The price of the contracts that have a longer expiry date will be quite high as compared to the ones with a shorter expiration date. It is based on the basic idea that a substantial movement in the value of the underlying security will mean that the extrinsic value of both sets of options will end up being equal or close to being full. The initial credit you receive is because of the higher extrinsic value of the options written. So, if the extrinsic value becomes equal on both sites, then that credit that will be created is your profits.

Chapter 17: How to Buy and Sell Puts

Let's talk about buying and selling puts. Puts, of course, allow you to sell the stock that you have or the underlying commodity that you have underneath it all. There are different reasons why people may want to buy or sell puts, and here we'll go over what it is, how to do it, and the advantages of such.

What are Buying and Selling Puts?

Selling/buying puts essentially is giving someone the option to buy the stock at a certain amount of money.

If you sell a put option, you're selling the chance for someone to buy that stock at a price.

If you buy a put option, you're giving someone the opportunity to buy that stock for that price and the person is obligated to sell it.

So, let's say that you're planning on getting a put option to buy that stock at a certain amount of money. You can put that option down, and from there, wait for it to fall, and from there, you can exercise it. Maybe you want to buy shares from an outstanding railroad company. You mainly notice it's increasing the earnings on this, and you decide to buy the stock when it's under 30 potentially. By purchasing a put option, basically makes the seller obligated to sell you the stock when it falls below 30 dollars.

You want to exercise these in falling markets since you'll generate a profit when the market is falling rather than rising.

Selling Puts in this Market

Here's the thing, when you want to sell puts, you should only do so if you're comfy with the owning stock that's under it at the price that's there because essentially, you're assuming the obligation to buy it if the person does decide to sell. From this, you should also only enter trades where the net price paid for the security is reasonable. This is the most crucial part of selling puts profitably in the markets that you have. There are other reasons to sell it to the person. You also can own the security below the market price that is currently there, and you'll definitely want to be careful when you do choose to sell this.

An Example of Buying a Put

Let us now move onto buying these puts. One thing to note is that you're not going to see the commissions, taxes, margins, and other charges factored into any of these equations for a reason. That starts to get it a bit more complicated, and right now, we are just showing you the cut and dry of all of the ways you can buy a put option that can be considered. But you should definitely consult with your tax advisor or broker before you go in.

So, let's say you've got company A, which is overvalued currently at $50 bucks a share, and you decide to bet on a decline at this point, getting a put contract that's at $35 a share, and it costs $2 per share, so the "breakeven" price is $33 a share. This is deduced from basic math since you're taking the contract price of 35 minus the 2 making it $33 for this. Since each of these represents 100 different shares, that's $3500 in a total of what you'll buy, and then of course, it'll cost you upfront $200 for this (cause of the options contract and the shares) and from there, you enter the trade.

Now, let's say that the option contract is for August 2019, and from there, you fast-forward and watch the market. Below is a table of what can happen:

Action of stock what happens to you your return Outlook

Soars all the way up to $60. The option expires, becomes worthless, and you lose the $200 premium, but you're basically losing nothing else (100%) Okay Falls slightly to $38. The same thing happens, stock falls but you don't make a profit (100%) Okay Drops all the way to $25 you make some cash! 800 dollars to be exact ($35-25) and then the $2 premium (800%) Nice! Drops to $0 (basically going bankrupt) the ideal situation, and you'll get $3300 from it (0 at expiration, so 3500-200 from the premium) (1500%) Ideal!

So, the best time to use these is when you have a sinking ship in terms of stock. Otherwise, they aren't worth your time, and it's better not to have these stocks, and there is always a chance you could end up losing money. But, if the person sells the capital, and you turn around and cash in on it, you'll have more money, and you don't have to worry about the burden of a stock.

If you choose to buy it when it declines, you're mostly going to get money from this. You want to do it when it's falling and nothing more. It is imperative that you don't choose to act on these types of options until it's that time.

That's it, that's all buying put options is, and you want to make sure that it falls to the level that you want it to be at.

The Risks of It

Risks are still there in both cases. Options are risky due to the complex nature of this, but once you know how these works, it can reduce the risk a whole lot. Put options, in particular, can be quite risky, especially for the seller, since they may have to spend more money buying back the opportunity that they once had.

One other aspect of this, especially for buyers is the break-even aspects of it. So, let's assume that you got a stock today for $46 and this was at $44, which is two points down what it is there, so you'll be profitable in the trade. But here's the thing, you're going to end up losing out on money due to the fee for the option. It would make the option worth $2 since you spent $4 on it, so that means you're losing out on it.

But there is also the fact that if the option does expire and you're in-the-money, you'll get the right stock immediately. You may not realize it, but these can be quite good, especially for plunging markets, especially if you know they will bounce back.

If you end up seeing it go high, you're going to end up paying for that premium to get the right to buy it, and that's money that can rack up to a couple of thousand dollars. Do make sure that you understand that when you do choose to figure out your own stock, and how you can quickly rectify it.

The Advantages of Buying Puts

Buying puts, which give you an option to sell the stock at a given price, is useful if you're looking to protect yourself. So, let's say that you have this stock, or you've been eyeing a share that will probably fall, and then rise over the ensuing few months. There are those out there, and usually, it's due to lulls in the market at the time. So, you decide to buy the put that's there, which gives you the option to sell that stock when the market decides to resurface at a higher level.

For you, you're taking a gamble on this, because the market may not recover, but if you notice a stock that could potentially have the power to fall possibly, this may be a good one. That way, you can get the share for cheaper. From there, you can sell the stock again, and you have the right to sell that stock at the price that you're looking for.

It essentially allows you to form that extra security in his, which is a great little advantage for the person who wants to sell it. Long puts are suitable for this, especially if you're going to sell these.

Put options let you sell this asset at the strike price that's there. With this, the seller is then obligated to purchase these shares from the holder. Now, how can this help? Let's say that you buy a stock at 20 bucks, and then you compare it to 20 dollars at the edge that's there. If the price is below 20 at any point, you can actually then exercise the options and reduce the losses. This can definitely help, especially if you're willing to buy a choice, and from there, sell it in order to avoid lots of trouble.

Naked Puts

There are also naked puts, which is an advanced put options strategy, so I don't suggest trying this until you've worked with basic puts. The reason for that is because of their incredibly risky.

What does it mean to trade an option naked though? It doesn't mean that you're going to the stock exchange in the buff, but rather, you're selling the options without having a position in the underlying instrument. For example, if you're writing a naked put, you're selling a put without having the stock.

The covered call is probably the most basic stock trading strategy. This strategy provides an ideal entry point for those who are new to options trading and allows them to turn their existing investment activities into a gateway for trading options. The premise of the covered call is quite simple. The idea behind this strategy is to minimize your cost basis on your stock purchases.

Let's take a look at how this works.

Covered Call Strategy

The best way to think about a covered call is to look at it as a method to earn dividends on your stock holdings. While a stock may or may not pay you a profit, with a covered call strategy you can earn income on the position and therefore lower your valid purchase price. Another way of looking at this is to view it as turning your stock purchase into a bond that pays you monthly or bi-monthly interest.

So how does it work? Well, the strategy has two legs to it.

- A long stock
- A short call

Execution

The long stock leg is simply your investment purchase in a stock. A lot of people who get into trading already hold shares as part of a retirement account or some other portfolio. If you already own a position in some stock, then employing this strategy will work wonders for you.

The execution is pretty straightforward. You already hold great stock or establish a long stock position in some company that you think has good long-term prospects. I must emphasize that this leg is all about investment and it has nothing to do with speculation. Whatever research you do to purchase this stock should be done on the basis of sound investment principles. So, you need to be aware of the earning ability of the company and its long-term prospects. Do not purchase a stock just to execute a covered call.

The short call simply provides short-term income against your long-term holding. So really, it's an appendage to the original position and gives you some cash in the short term while you're invested for the long-term capital gain. I know I'm repeating myself here, but this is because a lot of beginners think a covered call is a speculative strategy.

Chapter 18: Strategies for New Options Traders

There is no perfect trading strategy; so, stop searching for one. Moreover, you do not need a perfect trading strategy to make money from trading stocks. Ultimately, your trading strategy will be unique to you. However, as a beginner, you may need to lean a bit on an existing strategy to get the hang of it. With time, you can tweak things around to fit your trading style or build yours completely from scratch.

Here is a general idea you can use to build your own trading strategy.

Preparation

You could start preparing for your trade at the beginning of a new week. Find out what types of trade (short or long) you will want to focus on. You could use a technical indicator such as the moving averages to determine this. After that, look at a few financial columns or news, reports, etc. This will give you a general outlook of how stocks are performing and what the market is up to. Look at charts of various industries to see stock strengths and weaknesses, plus promising stocks. Be sure to write down whatever catches your attention in your trading notepad (you don't have one yet?) because in the heat of trading, most things you note mentally won't come to your mind.

Finding Stocks

- Begin to search for potential trades by looking for stocks that:
- Have a strong trend
- Have shown first pullbacks or rallies
- Are at a resistance or support level
- Are in the second or fourth stages
- Are repeatedly touching a support or resistance area

If you do not find a trade that you are comfortable with as a beginner, please do not trade. Remember, trading involves going long, short, or staying in cash. So, learn to stay in cash if there is nothing appealing for you to trade.

Double-Check

After you have found a trade, verify that the company whose stock you are about to trade will not release its earnings reports anytime soon. Trading a company's stock just before their earnings report is released can lead to a massive loss for you. So be sure to double-check. Here's one way you could find out. Simply go to Yahoo Finance and type in the company's symbol. The date of the next earnings report will be shown.

During Trades

All things checked and verified, start your trade. Do not give your attention to stock market news or other trader's opinions during your own trades. Your attention needs to be only in one place: the stock chart. Ensure that you use trailing stops to follow your profits closely and that would be all you require during trades.

Your Entry Strategy

Your money is at risk as soon as you enter a position to buy or sell a stock.

So, you must be careful that you time your entry very well.

Your entry point should be at a swing point: a low swing point for buying, and a high swing point for selling.

A swing point is made up of three candles.

Low Swing Point (for entering a long position – buying)

1. Candle one goes low
2. Candle two goes lower than candle one (lower low)
3. Candle three goes higher than candle two (higher low)

Candle three indicates that sellers are no more aggressive. This is a precursor for a trend reversal. This is your cue to enter a long position.

High Swing Point (for entering a short position – selling)

1. Candle one goes high
2. Candle two goes higher than candle one (higher high)
3. Candle three goes lower than candle two (lower high)

Candle three indicates that buyers are no more aggressive. This is a precursor for a trend reversal. This is your cue to enter a short position.

Successive Up Days or Down Days

Another way to enter a trade is to look for successive up days or down days. These are a lot easier to spot but be sure that you are not entering the trade when the trend is about to end or reverse.

Your Exit Strategy

You have read all the charts and picked your stocks to trade and you have determined which market to trade on—in fact, you know exactly when to time your entry. But when do you exit a trade? When do you lock in profits? You see, as important as timing your entry is, if you neglect when to exit, you may not take any profits home after all.

You must plan well ahead of your entry how you intend to exit a trade. And remember that a plan is not a plan until it is written down. Following a plan in your head is the same as trading based on your emotions. It usually fails. Basically, there're three reasons why you should exit a trade, namely: when making profits, when losing money, and when you are not making or losing money.

Let us take a brief look at each of these reasons for exiting a trade.

Taking Your Profits

Before you enter a trade, it is important to set a mechanism that tells you it is time to take your profits and exit the trade. Do not rely on some abstract feelings. Remember to be emotionally detached from your trade outcomes.

That way, you will pay more attention to your formerly set mechanism when it alerts you of an exit point. If you are greedy and wait too long, you may lose a substantial part of your profits and if you are too fearful and quit too soon, you may equally lose a significant part of profits that should be yours. This boils down to emotional intelligence.

The good news is that it can be developed. So, if you intend to become a successful swing trader and you have determined that you do not have enough discipline to follow through with your plan, do not worry. You can learn how to do that as you take baby steps in options trading.

When you buy or sell a stock, ensure that you have a stop-loss point in mind. You can use that point to set a stop-loss order, or you can click buy or sell when prices get to that point.

Ending Your Losses

Make up your mind long before you enter any trade that you are going to cut your losses early enough before it digs a hole in your account that will require a lot of money to mend. Again, you must set up a prior mechanism for identifying when to cut your losses. I strongly suggest that you use the trailing stops to cut losses. Set your losses to somewhere around 3% (or less) of your capital. Make your losses as small as possible so you don't get all emotional about the loss.

Be on the lookout for repeated price attempts to breach support or resistance. That is an indication of a possible breakout. Sticking to a losing position in the hope of it rebounding is abandoning your plans and listening to your emotions. In options trading, hope doesn't give you profits. Most often than not, hope has an ironic way of crippling your account.

Freeing Up Your Capital

Whether you choose to quickly exit a trade that is neither making you money nor making you lose money, or you choose to watch it for a few days, both choices are okay. The important thing is that before you enter the trade, you should make up your mind about how long you are willing to watch a trade that is generally lukewarm.

Remember that you are in a type of trade that is considered short-term. You don't have the whole month to wait for one position. If it is tying down your money, free up your capital and reinvest it in another stock or position.

Trading Pullbacks and Rallies

Usually, when stock prices begin to move upward (an uptrend), they tend to pull back briefly. This presents you a good opportunity to buy at low risk and increases your chances of selling at a higher price later. On the reverse side, when stock prices begin to move in a downward direction (downtrend), they tend to rally briefly and offer you an excellent opportunity for shorting.

Here's something for you to consider as a beginner in options trading. If all you do is simply stay in cash (that is, holding on to your money without trading) until you find excellent pullbacks and rallies, you will be making a wise beginner decision.

Think about it. It is known that one of the best times to buy stocks at a great price is right after a recent occurrence of selling. It equally shows better judgment to short sell right after the occurrence of buying.

The best time to trade pullbacks and rallies is the first time they appear on a chart after a significant trend. So, the first time you notice a pullback after a trend line is breached or broken, seize the opportunity.

Buy or sell at that point. When you see a breakout, be ready to trade the first pullback after it. When a new high is set, wait for the first pullback. When it comes up, go in for the kill.

Let us look at the chart below to get a clearer picture of the above. The first pullback after a significant downtrend offered those who were watchful an excellent opportunity to buy early.

You Cannot Win All Trades

No, you can't. It doesn't matter what tools or magic formula you use. Remember that the stock market contains so many moving parts that are far beyond the control of anyone individual or a body. Any of these moving parts could have a significant adverse effect on even the best technical indicators or analysis tools.

But you can win a lot of trades enough to make you good profits. The profits you make come from the ignorance or mistakes of other traders. In the stock market, you are either making mistakes or you are making profits. Unfortunately, for most traders, they are making mistakes. Whether you will choose to make profits depends largely on if you will take your learning seriously to avoid the mistakes most novices make.

Some of these mistakes are depending 100% on technical analysis, being too afraid to lose, looking for a fail-proof system or trading magic formula, being emotional, etc. Not really everyone is cut out to be a trader or a swing trader. However, a lot of people will give it a shot and eventually fail. From these failed attempts, you will make profits if you learn and apply what these other traders won't.

Chapter 19: Risk Management

When you are trading in options, managing your risk in the right way is essential to keep your capital safe. In certain forms of investments, you will come across a situation where exposure to risk is totally unavoidable, and at that time, you have to remind yourself that it is not the exposure to risk that poses the problem but the poor management of risk. Risks will always be there but what you need to keep in mind is that you are not incurring unsustainable losses.

I will introduce you to various ways in which you can manage your risk and also bring home good profits.

Practice Optimal Position Sizing

Position sizing is the first step to effective risk management. Managing risk and managing money are two things that are very closely related to each other. Remember that the amount of money you have in hand is limited, and so, keep track of your budget is vital so that you don't end up losing all your capital. When you learn the concept of position sizing, managing your money becomes easier. The term basically refers to the amount of capital that a trader is using to enter any specific position in the market. Most beginner traders think that position sizing does not require any special planning and can be done randomly, but that is not how it works.

They often think that if they are really confident about a trade, then they can choose a larger position size, and if they are a bit less confident, then a small position size would be apt. But this is not at all a strategic way to approach it.

So, the most effective way of determining the position size is first to figure out how much capital you want to invest in each trade, and then you also need to find out how much that capital is in terms of percentage of your total capital. If you think about it carefully, you will realize that position sizing is not that much different from the concept of diversification. The idea is to allow only a very small percentage of your capital to any single trade, and by doing this, you are risking only a very specific small amount of money. The key aspect here is to ensure that one bad trade does not affect your total capital.

Let us say almost 50% of your total capital has been put into one single trade, and then, you end up losing that trade, then in just one trade, a significant portion of your capital is lost. That is why it is said that you should risk only 1% of your total capital in one trade. This will ensure that even if you had a number of consecutive losses, your overall capital is not affected.

Never Risk More Than You Can Afford to Lose

The consequences of losing the entire capital or most parts of your capital are quite bad. Your aim should be keeping the risk really low, and so, you should not use that much, which you cannot afford to lose. Make a monthly budget and find out what your monthly expenses are. Then keep some money aside for your retirement plan, and then you can set aside money for trading capital. Never use the money for monthly expenses into trading. Similarly, you should not invest your entire trading capital in a single trade.

Stick to Your Trading Plan

It might sound simple to you know how it is a big task to stick to the trading plan, but it is a big task. Some people lose sight of the fact while trading and deviate from the plan. That is when they step into a territory of uncertainty and end up making bad decisions.

Always Have an Exit Plan

One of the important steps of managing risk in options trading is to learn to have an exit plan. There are plenty of variables in this type of trading that you cannot have control over; that is why before you enter a trade, your exit plan should be in place.

Now, what is an exit plan? There are two major things that must be included in an exit plan, and they are:

- If things are not working in your favor, then at what point are you going to get out of the trade?
- If things do work in your favor, then when are you going to take the profits and exit the trade?

Now, if the market conditions don't work out and options become extremely volatile, then you should have a fixed percentage of fluctuation that you would tolerate before getting out of the trade. If 30-50% of the capital invested is already lost, it is time for you to exit the trade before you lose everything. Swallow the losses, learn from your mistakes, and start afresh.

But if things do work out in your favor, then your aim would be to keep your profits safe. The take profit point is a tricky thing, and it usually differs depending on the market condition. You will learn to set this with more precision as you gain more experience in the market.

Every trader spends a lot of time devising their entry strategies, and they forget that if they do not exit the market at the right time, then all their profits would be lost. But an experienced trader always has an exit strategy ready. Even if your entry into the trade was terrible, if you exit it in the right manner, you can be saved. But if your entry was perfect and your exit was wrong, then it can do more harm than good. Also, another thing to keep in mind is figuring out what your maximum potential losses are.

Be Smart While Using Options Spreads

These are some of the most powerful tools you have in the realm of options trading, so you know that these strategies involve the usage of more than one position on options contracts where the underlying stock or asset remains the same.

The spreads are very special because they give you an effective chance to manage your risk. When you are entering a position, you can significantly reduce your upfront costs with the help of these spreads. Also, you can reduce the amount of money you stand to lose in a trade with the help of spreads. The bull call spread is a perfect example of that. In this strategy, your potential for profit does reduce a bit, but in doing so, you are also minimizing your overall risk.

If you want to enter a short position, even then, the proper use of spreads can minimize the risk involved. In both cases, you will be entering the positions with the aim that even if the prices don't go as planned, you still stand to gain some money. This is why spreads are considered to be an excellent strategy for risk management and are used by most options traders. They can also be used in pretty much every market condition.

Diversify

You must have heard of diversification as a risk management strategy whenever we talk about the stock market and mostly when people are into the buy and hold strategy. The basic idea of diversification is that you spread your investments over a wide range of companies and sectors so that you don't have a lot of money tied to any company or sector. But what about options trading? Diversification does not work in the same way here, but you cannot deny the different risk management benefits it has.

In options trading, you can engage in diversification by trading in options that have different types of underlying assets. The ultimate idea remains the same—you are not relying on any single type of security for your profits but diversifying your trades. But this was only one way of diversification, that is, across products.

You can also diversify your trades based on direction. This means you have to ensure that your directional risk has not accumulated on one side. You should have some neutral trades, some bearish trades, and some bullish trades. And lastly, you should also diversify by time. The expiration cycles of your options should be different. This will ensure that their volatility and changes in stock prices are different.

Cover Short Options Soon

Traders often make the mistake of waiting for a long period of time before they can buy back their short options, but you always need to be ready and attentive about them. It is quite natural for you to think that since the trade is going the way you wanted, you can now rest and take a break, but you have to keep in mind that this will not always be the case. Sometimes, trades can quickly start to move in the opposite direction.

If things change all of a sudden and you don't notice, there can be a million excuses for you to give, but nothing will get you back your lost profits.

So, if you notice that your short option is going too much out-of-the-money, then don't think twice before buying it back. Do it now and reduce the risk from your plate. If you are thinking about the profits, then here is something that you should follow—if about 80% or more of your initial profit from the sale of the option stays with you, then don't worry, and buy the option now. Otherwise, if you wait too long, the same short option might come back and be a headache for you.

Chapter 20: The Greeks

One of the things you need to learn about and be aware of when it comes to options trading is the "Greeks." These are parameters with Greek letters that will help you estimate the future behavior of options pricing. So, you need to keep them in mind when considering getting into a trade and exiting your trades. There are five of these parameters in total. They are delta, theta, gamma, rho, and Vega. In most cases, delta and theta are what you need to pay attention to, and the rest are details. As we will see, in today's environment where interest rates are low and not changing by very much, rho isn't of much relevance. But, of course, you should be aware of what rho means because, at some point in the future, interest rates may rise higher or become more volatile.

Vega has some relevance in relation to the volatility of a stock. Most of the time, it's not that important, but as we'll see, there are certain situations when it can impact options prices significantly, and there are strategies that you can use to profit from this.

For the most part, options traders need to be focused on delta and theta. Understanding these two parameters can help you be more aware and effective in your options trading. They will help you to be more informed when it comes to the prospects of a given options contract, and where it is going once you've invested in it. A more informed trader is always going to be a more successful trader, and those who do their trading on the fly are usually the same people that end up with heavy losses.

Delta

The first Greek that we are going to look at is one of the most important. The main piece of information that you are going to get from the delta is the amount that the price of an option is going to change in reaction to the given change of the underlying stock's price. Delta is expressed as a fraction, so it can be viewed as giving you the percentage by which the price of the option will change as a fraction of the change in the stock price. Or you can just look at it in terms of change by a dollar in the stock's price.

Looking at a $235 strike call option on Apple, the delta is 0.5427. So that means there is going to be about a 54 cent change in the price of the option for every dollar price change in Apple stock. You will recall that earlier; we mentioned that there is a rule of thumb for an at-the-money option—it will change by 50 cents for every dollar change in the price of the underlying stock. This proves the point that the option is about $1 in the money, which is barely in the money—and it's going to change by 54 cents, which is quite close to the 50 cent value.

Delta is not a fixed value. You will see it change in real-time as the stock price moves up and down. Of course, in most circumstances, the delta is not going to change very much over a relatively short time period, like a day or so. But you need to be aware that when you go look up the delta and see that it is a specific value, that value is dynamic and not fixed, so you need to keep your eye on how it's changing.

Theta

The second Greek that you want to pay close attention to is called theta. This gives you a relatively precise estimate of the time decay of the option. Theta is expressed as a negative value, which is an indication that it will decrease in value for each passing day. Theta is dynamic like delta, but it will be changing by small amounts in the entire day of trading as long as there is a change in the value of the price of the stock. The main point at which theta becomes important is with turnover. That is, options prices drop at market open due to value lost through time decay. And guess how much they drop? Take theta and multiply it by 100. So, if theta is -0.11, that means that the price of the option is going to automatically drop by $11 when the market opens the next day.

Theta is going to have higher values, the closer the option is to be at the money. Theta has smaller values when options are more in the money, but it also has smaller values when options are more out of the money.

But rather than worrying about the variation, you need to be aware of the value of the theta for any option that you invest in. This way, you can consider the amount of money you are going to lose if you hold any option overnight.

This will have to be considered along with many other factors, of course. But, in some cases, it is not going to be worth it to hold the option overnight and take the hit to the options price. If you have an option that is trading at $100, a theta value of -0.11 means that your option is going to lose 11% of its value overnight. Is that significant? It depends since a movement in share price can easily overwhelm that value. If you were trading call options, and the share price was to go up by 50 cents, with delta equal to say 0.65 that would indicate that the option's price would go up by $32.50 from the delta but drop by $11 from the theta. So, on the net, you'd be profiting. That means both values need to be considered, and you need to be on top of things as far as estimating how the stock is going to move.

Earlier, we mentioned that beginning options traders often make the mistake of holding losing trades all the way through expiration, and they end up losing their entire investment when they could have cut their losses. But there is another problem many beginning traders run into—and that is getting out too early when they should not do so. The above example might illustrate this, believe it or not, many new options traders will panic at the thought of time decay and sell their option before market close, and then the following morning even though the option starts out of the gate taking a hit because of the time decay-driven losses, it quickly recovers and becomes profitable due to a move in the underlying stock price.

Vega

The underlying volatility of a stock is an important factor influencing options prices. Volatility is a measure of how drastically stock prices are changing with time. If a stock has a median share price of $32, and it fluctuates between $30 and $34 over the course of a week, it is far less volatile than a stock that has a median share price of $32, but the second stock fluctuates between $25 and $50 over the same time period. So, volatility is a measure of how much change there is in a share price and how frequently it's changing. You can think of this in terms of graphics as well. A very jagged curve fluctuating up and down between wildly different values is very volatile, while a stable stock price that is practically a smooth line over the same time period is not very volatile.

One measure you can look for on your brokerage account or stock market sites is to look up the value of beta for a given company. Beta is a comparison of the stock's volatility relative to the market average. It is expressed as being greater or less than 1. The stock market average is normalized to 1.0. Any value greater than 1.0 indicates a highly volatile stock, while a value of less than 1.0 indicates a stock that is not very volatile.

If you look up a given stock, and you find that beta is 1.53 that means it's 53% more volatile than the market average. On the other hand, if you look up a stock and find that beta is 0.4, that means it's only 40% as volatile as the average. Beta is actually calculated using five-year averages.

The volatility of a stock really doesn't have anything to do with whether or not the stock is desirable to own as an investment. Some very highly desirable stocks have high beta values, but some have relatively low beta values.

Gamma

Gamma is one of the Greeks that get less attention, and it's a little more complicated, which might be one of the reasons that it's not tops on most people's lists. The value of paying much attention to it is not as clear cut either. Gamma is a quantity that gives you the rate of change of delta. It will tell you the amount of change in the value of delta you can expect when the stock price changes. Gamma values tend to be pretty small, on the order of 0.01-0.03 or so. For example, let the share price be $100, delta 0.65, and gamma 0.01. If the share price were to rise $1 that would mean that delta would rise to 0.66. If gamma had been 0.03, then the value of delta would have changed to 0.68 for the same $1 change in the share price.

Rho

The last of the Greeks is rho. We are leaving that to the end because these days, Rho is the least important of the Greeks. Rho is related to interest rates. Specifically, the value of rho is related to a hypothetical "risk-free" interest rate. It gives you an estimate of how the option's price would change relative to a one-point change in the risk-free interest rate. Since interest rates are not changing by large amounts in today's environment, this is not going to be a quantity that is going to require much attention.

So, what is the risk-free interest rate? This is an estimate of what the interest rate would be if you had your money in a risk-free investment. Interest rates for the past ten years have been at historic lows. Generally, the risk-free interest rate is taken to be the interest rate on a 10-year U.S. Treasury. That is about as close as you can get to a risk-free investment. You are pretty much guaranteed, at least for the time being, of getting your capital back if you invest in ten year U.S. government bonds.

Chapter 21: Algorithmic Trading

What is an Algorithm?

"An algorithm is a set of unambiguous instructions for performing a task. Algorithms can execute automatically (as in a computer program) or manually (as in an unautomated process). An algorithm has inputs and outputs."

The term "algorithm" is derived from the name of Persian mathematician Abū Ja'far Muhammad ibn Mūsā al-Khwārizmī, often Latinized as "Algoritmi" and called "the father of algorithmic art". He wrote several treatises on the Hindu-Arabic numeral system in the 9th century, but most of them have not survived.

What is Algorithmic Trading?

Algorithmic trading is a method of executing a large order (too large to fill all at once) using automated pre-programmed trading instructions accounting for variables such as time, price, and volume to send small slices of the order (child orders) out to the market over time.

Algorithmic Trading is the set of rules and procedures used by investors or their advisors to issue orders automatically based on certain pre-defined parameters.

Why Use Algorithmic Trading?

The idea behind algorithmic trading is to use advanced computer algorithms to reduce human irrationality and emotions. The benefits of automated trading are numerous and include:

- Reduction in trading costs - by placing many orders at once, the market impact cost of each individual trade is significantly decreased.
- Reduction in Capital Requirements - by executing a large order over time, you can often invest more with less capital.
- More flexibility - since algorithmic traders are not bound to pre-determined schedules, they can execute trades based on immediate market conditions. This provides investors with improved liquidity and the ability to respond quickly to changing markets.

Algorithmic trading systems are used in every major financial market around the world, including stocks, futures, foreign exchange (forex), options, bonds, and commodities.

Working of Algorithmic Trading System:

The algorithmic trading system works on a mathematical algorithm based on the commonly available market data. The algorithmic trading system is a set of rules that are fully automated by the computer-based program. It means no human involvement in the whole trading process. The software monitors the market continuously and makes automated decisions about when to buy or sell shares or other financial instruments.

An algorithmic trading systems program sets the rules and monitors the market for opportunities to take advantage of. It can place bids and offers on your behalf in a fast and efficient manner.

How Algorithmic Trading System Works?

The algorithmic trading system works on a mathematical algorithm based on the commonly available market data. The traders set the mathematical equations before they are fed into a computer, which then decides when to buy or sell shares or other financial instruments on their behalf based on pre-programmed instructions.

The trader may define simple entry and exit rules or more complex pricing models to execute the trades.

Algo Trading can be done in one of two ways: direct or indirect.

Note: The Methods used for Algorithmic Trading may be either Manual or Semi-Automatic, where the trader makes the decision and then the computer executes the trade, however, in a fully automated system such as ADL (Automated Delivery of Liquidity) by Comex, there is no human intervention at all. In an ADL system, a client can simply connect their trading platform to that of Comex and allow their orders to be automatically executed by the ADL system with no intervention on their part whatsoever.

The indirect method uses the data feeds from stock exchanges to find out the real-time value of the shares. Based on this information and by using specific pre-programmed rules, an algorithm can then decide when to buy or sell shares. This is basically how all online brokers operate.

The direct method involves two parts: The first is the monitoring of data feeds from stock exchanges and other sources of information, and an algorithm analyzing this data to decide whether to buy or sell shares based on pre-defined instructions. The second part is a direct connection with the stock exchange through a dedicated line (leased line) where child orders are sent directly to the exchange without passing through an online broker's computer system. This method is slower than the indirect method because it involves the transmission of orders through a leased line and the response for execution is received after a small delay. However, some firms use this method as they are worried about their online brokers using their algorithms and information to trade against them.

How to Start Algo Trading?

It's not easy to start algorithmic trading. It involves purchasing some software and hiring some people with the necessary skills. However, one can outsource it if he wants to do algorithmic trading on a small scale. Some financial service companies, for example, sell pre-programmed trading algorithms (generally called "systems") that investors can use with their own money. Most of these systems can be used to trade a variety of assets, including stocks, options and futures. Some systems trade only one asset such as gold or silver.

However, not all algorithmic trading is done by big institutions with teams of people and lots of capital. Non-professional algorithmic traders are generally known as "retail algorithmic traders" because they use their own money to fund their trading operations. These individual investors often enter trades manually, but use algorithmic trading software for "dealing" with the execution of specific trades, such as placing orders on the buy and sell sides simultaneously in order to capture the spread.

Other than that, in order to automate your algorithmic trading system; you need the following:

1. An Internet connection
2. A trading platform (this can be an individual software or a service that can connect you with the financial exchanges)
3. An Algorithm (this is basically a set of instructions that tell your computer when to buy or sell shares or other financial instruments).
4. Financial Market Data (to see how the market is performing and where there may be opportunities to trade)
5. A Broker (to execute trades with your broker and provide you with market data)

6. Risk Management and Money management (This is basically the backtesting part of it. Backtesting involves running a simulation on historical data to see how profitable your algorithm could have been).

Pros and Cons of Algorithmic Trading

There are both pros and cons in algorithmic trading. Here are some of them:

Benefits: Algorithmic trading is very advantageous because it can be done 24 hours a day, 365 days a year without requiring any human intervention.

It is generally faster than a manual trader, and more reliable since it performs error checks and can recover from system failure or other interruptions to a trading session.

It is cost effective in terms of labor cost. A computer doesn't get tired of doing the same job for hours on end, a human being does. This means that it's cheaper to pay a computer to trade for you all day long rather than paying an employee that will get tired doing it.

Algorithmic trading requires lower investment capital as compared to human discretionary traders.

Drawbacks: The software that comes with algorithmic trading may not be perfect and can make mistakes resulting in losses in the portfolio.

It is important to note that the Algo Trading Software may not be able to handle large market movements and an unexpected crash in the market can result in a devastating loss for the trader.

Since algorithmic trading uses logic to make decisions based on prices, there is no room for emotions which could result in poor decision-making.

Despite this, as an individual trader using these methods, I find them very useful because they allow me to see opportunities I wouldn't have noticed otherwise or perform analysis on my trade ideas very quickly. That way, you get all the advantages of automated trading without any of its drawbacks.

Conclusion

Trading options involves a selection of considerations both before as well as after the trade has been placed. Many of the mistakes mentioned may be accounted for before the trade is opened through the use of the tools and materials. The one most significant step to trading options is developing a scheme as well as stick with it!

In this book, you find several of the equipment as well as materials that will help you build your plan. Make use of these along with other trading programs and resources Fidelity offers to allow you to stay away from these typical choices trading mistakes.

Once again, day trading is not for everybody. However, based upon hard-won, individual experience, this book provides you with the details you require to see if day trading is an excellent individual option for you on your journey to monetary liberty and security.

This manual offers you the type of standard detailed details you've been trying to find to make an educated choice about day trading. Make no error about it; this kind of speculative stock trading is not for everybody. By setting out the procedure you require to go through in a practical and useful method, you get a clear concept of precisely what you'll be entering when you begin day trading.

Far from dissuading or downhearted, it also provides a practical and well-balanced view of what it's like to prepare to trade, in addition to the truths you'll deal with when you day trade. You get vital pointers on the state of minds you require to embrace, the tools you need to get, crucial strategies effective and reliable day traders utilize, and directions on how to establish your extremely own effective individual day-trading method.

You are looking at the best manuscript if you are a total rookie to day trading and desire the within dope or straight talk about this kind of securities trading. Rather of investing an excessive quantity of time and volume area on just how much you can make from day trading, in addition to the monetary liberty you can delight in, this manuscript focuses the majority of its firepower on what you require to understand so you can be successful with day trading.

One of my favorite things about options is that you can get involved in options trading without having much money. If people were smart and disciplined about it, options trading could even provide a way out of a low-income situation. You can start trading with a hundred dollars, and if you are careful with it a year from now, there is no reason that you could not significantly grow that into a large trading account.

Just remember that options trading is a serious business, but it can be fun and exciting too. There is no reason why making money has to be tedious and difficult. You can get involved at the highest levels of our economy with the best companies by trading options. You will be able to go by on the stock market and earn some of your profits.

www.ingramcontent.com/pod-product-compliance
Lightning Source LLC
Chambersburg PA
CBHW071411210526
45465CB00001B/332